Shout It from the Housetops

Shout It from the Housetops

by PAT ROBERTSON

with Jamie Buckingham

LOGOS INTERNATIONAL
PLAINFIELD, NEW JERSEY
1972

There is nothing covered up
That will not be uncovered,
Nothing hidden
That will not be made known.
What I say to you in the dark
You must repeat in broad daylight;
What you hear whispered
You must shout from the housetops.

—Matthew 10:26,27 (NEB)

Contents

Preface

In the early months of 1968 I received a letter from Irene Harrell. Irene, a very fine writer and wife of a North Carolina judge, had just heard Pat Robertson speak at a Full Gospel meeting.

"God has told me that you are supposed to write a book about Pat Robertson, President of the Christian Broadcasting Network in Portsmouth, Virginia," she wrote.

I looked at the brochure she enclosed. There was a picture of Pat, looking for all the world like the late President John F. Kennedy. On the back was a list of the impossible goals he had set up for CBN—starting with carrying the Gospel to all the world via broadcasting.

I remembered how I used to make fun of the bad-grammared radio preacher who came on at 5:15 every morning over a 150-watt station in the Carolina piedmont. His shouting voice reached out barely five miles to a handful of chicken farmers as he signed on with a nasal twang: "HELLO, WORLD!"

I shook my head and stuffed Irene's letter and the brochure in my filing cabinet. Christian broadcasting, to me, consisted of some whiney-voiced evangelist saying, "Keep those cards and letters coming, folks." And as for Pat's dream of reaching the entire world for Christ via radio and television, well . . .

But I was wrong—about Pat and about his dream. And two years later as I stepped off a jet in Bogota, Colombia, to begin my interviews with him, I realized just how wrong I had been. For this was not just Pat's story: it was the story of any man who ventured into business for (and with) God; it was the story of any man who dared to walk by faith and not by sight.

Somewhere, about halfway through the manuscript, I began to compare my own lack of faith with Pat's willingness to risk all for

Jesus. Unable to continue typing, I sat there thinking of God's challenge to me—and my reluctance to follow it. I picked up a felt-tipped pen and wrote down what I heard God saying, not only to me but to all others who dare to step out with him: "ATTEMPT SOMETHING SO BIG, THAT UNLESS GOD INTERVENES, IT IS BOUND TO FAIL!" I stuck it on the wall over my typewriter where it still hangs.

I resumed my typing on the manuscript. But for the first time I was able to look out my window, beyond the housetops that had formerly limited my vision, and shout with all those who walk by faith, "HELLO, WORLD!"

JAMIE BUCKINGHAM
Melbourne, Florida

Introduction

Have you ever wondered, "Suppose the rich young ruler whom Jesus called had made a different choice—if, instead of turning away sorrowful, he had sold all that he had to follow Jesus? What would have happened to him? What would he have become?"

It would have been something very special, we can be sure, because he was a very special young man. He is one of the two men in all the Gospels whom, we are specifically told, "Jesus loved."

Actually I think I have a clue as to what could have happened to him. I find it in the life of a friend of mine, a rich young ruler who did not turn away sorrowful, but hilariously sold all that he had to follow Jesus.

I don't know how much money Pat Robertson has now—not very much I suppose—but I do know that he grew up rich in all the things that make for what the world calls "success." The family background, the Ivy League education, the talent and ambition—he had them all; but when he found the pearl of great price, he "sold" them all to possess it! And now, in the real sense, he is one of the richest men I know. I think, as you read this story, he will enrich you as he has me and millions of others.

The son of a distinguished U.S. Senator, Pat Robertson has that ruggedly handsome, aristocratic charm, the boyish winsomeness and personal charisma that carried the Kennedys so far and so high in the political arena; but like Paul, when he met the Lord, those things that were gain to him he counted as worthless for the prize of the high call of God in Christ Jesus.

This personal account of what happened before and since Pat's great encounter, makes very, very exciting reading. More important, it will put a yearning in your heart—I hope greater than ever before —to go all out, at whatever the cost, to follow Jesus, the Son of God.

PAT BOONE

[xi]

Shout It from the Housetops

I

Something's Missing

———
———
———

"The minister came to call today." Dede grinned mischievously as I walked through the front door of our little Staten Island cottage.

"Oh no," I groaned. "What did he have to say?"

She brushed her auburn hair away from her pretty face and continued folding the huge pile of diapers on the sofa. "Not much, really. It was the look on his face. He was completely shattered."

I glanced up at the print of the huge nude by Modigliani hanging over the sofa and remembered how funny it had seemed when we sat around drinking and laughing and Dede's father had quipped, "If you kids ever get hungry, you can live off that hunk of beef for a month." It wasn't funny now, and I groaned again.

Actually our home was a chauffeur's cottage on an estate overlooking the New York Harbor. It seemed to be the perfect place for us to live if we were to build our image as sophisticated New York swingers who were rapidly climbing the success ladder. The room was wildly decorated, reflecting our jet-set tastes. The inside walls were painted copper, and the woodwork was charcoal and white. Dede and I had worked tediously to cover the furniture with charcoal corduroy to match the trim, and a couple of weird contour chairs gave the room an ultra-mod look. The burlap curtains on the windows lent the feeling of intimacy, but dominating the scene was the huge orange and red nude.

Dede continued, "I had just come in from the laundromat and put

[1]

Tim down for his nap when this man walked in. He just stood there looking—as if he didn't know where to look."

"Well, what did you say?"

"I didn't know what to say. I've never had a minister come calling before. So I told him you were going into the ministry."

I collapsed into one of the contour chairs. "Oh no!"

"Don't worry." She chuckled as she gathered up an armload of diapers and started into the other room. "I don't think he even heard me. I tried to be nice but he just stood there wide-eyed, staring. Besides, about that time Tim came wandering down the steps stark naked, and the poor man just backed out of the door and disappeared."

Suddenly I saw the room through his eyes. The risqué de Maupassant stories, the Courvoisier brandy, the far-out decor, and finally the picture. All the things we thought were so big-time, now seemed somehow empty.

Dede was gone now to get ready for dinner. It gave me a moment to reflect. Things just didn't seem to be adding up. My father, as U.S. Senator from Virginia and chairman of the Banking and Currency Committee, was one of the most powerful men in the nation. I had a proud Southern heritage—honor grad from military prep school, Golden Gloves boxer, Phi Beta Kappa at Washington and Lee, Marine combat officer in Korea, law degree from Yale, trouble-shooter for the W. R. Grace Company in South America, and now in the electronic component business with some of my old law school buddies. And on top of it all, 1956 was an election year, and I was chairman of the Stevenson-for-President campaign headquarters on Staten Island. Yet suddenly it all seemed empty. What was the matter with me?

I sat there, looking absently at the ceiling and hearing Dede moving about in the kitchen. Another of those strange feelings that had been clouding up my thoughts with increasing frequency for the past year settled over me. *God has a purpose for your life.* An inaudible voice seemed to be speaking in the deep recesses of my mind.

God.

The only other person I knew who really felt this way was my mother. In her long, involved, and often preachy letters from Lexington, she constantly reminded me she was praying for me. "Pat, God has a plan for your life, and you will never be happy until you are in the center of that plan."

God? Who was he, really? I had joined our Southern Baptist Church in Lexington as a boy—just like all the other boys. But the experiences had been primarily social, not spiritual. Time was spent in Sunday school and church—but I never did really understand what the church was all about. It had been so easy to drop away from it when I left home.

It wasn't that I had pushed God out of my thoughts. I had always been uneasily aware that one day I would have to come to terms with him, but it just never seemed like quite the right time.

One night, a few months before, I had prayed, "All right, God. Let me make my fortune, and then I'll lay my money at your feet and become a philanthropist. I'll give all my money away for the good of mankind."

Somehow or other, though, I had a hunch God wasn't pleased with my offer. It was almost as if making a lot of money kept people away from the deep purposes of God, rather than being the key to open the door. Inside, I knew God would never be satisfied until I gave him my all. But how? That was the question.

Dede poured me a drink and then returned to the kitchen to make the last-minute preparations for dinner. We had met at Yale where she was working on her master's degree in nursing, and we had married before I finished school. Yet, even in marriage I was so burdened with the futility of life that at one point I had actually contemplated suicide.

After graduation I had taken the New York bar exam, but my heart was not in it, and I had failed. My father was perplexed, heartbroken. "Pat, you've always made your mark; there's been nothing out of your reach. Now you fail the bar exam. What's wrong?"

I doubted seriously if I could ever explain to Dad the disillusionment I felt about life. I had tried pleasure, philosophy, a profession—nothing satisfied. I lived with a nagging feeling I just didn't belong anywhere. Life was empty.

The only real contact I had with any purpose in life came through Mother's letters. She was lonely and wrote often. Dad stayed in Washington during the week, getting home only on weekends. But Mother was a gracious, charming woman who kept mostly to herself —and God. She bombarded us with Gospel literature until Dede felt that she was a religious fanatic, and I tossed the letters aside. Yet I knew they were not empty forms, but an extension of the very life she lived.

Late one night after Dede had put Tim in the little upstairs bedroom, she joined me on the sofa in the front room. She was putting on fresh pillowcases before we pulled out the sofa bed for the night, and I blurted out, "You know, I really feel God wants me to go into the ministry."

I waited for her reaction. There was none.

"Well, what do you think?"

"I think it might be fun," she said, sitting down beside me. "Maybe you could get a nice church, and I could sit behind a beautiful silver tea service and entertain. We could have a big old manse with rooms to spare. It sounds exciting."

It was exciting to me, too, but for different reasons. I wasn't making much of a contribution to the world as it was, and obviously the world situation was not getting better. If it were to be saved, it would take men for whom money was not a prime motivation—men ready to live and die to help people. And what better way to help people, I thought, than by being a minister.

Dede looked at me. "I guess if you're going to think seriously about going in the ministry, we ought to start going to church and find out what it's all about," she ventured.

It was a good idea, and for the last several Sundays we had been visiting various churches. Since I was a Baptist, we started out there.

On our way home from church that first Sunday I asked Dede, whose background was Roman Catholic, what she thought of the service.

"I'm puzzled," she said. "Why did that man get up in the middle of the service and start blowing that horrible horn?"

"Oh, that was just a trumpet solo," I explained. "What did you think of the sermon?"

"It wasn't a very good sermon either," she said. "I thought Catholics were the only ones who read out of books. He read the whole thing. But that horn was enough for me," she said, shuddering. "Let's try someplace else next week."

The next week we attended a Moravian Church. It was Communion Sunday, and they had the "right hand of fellowship." In fact, they had it about six times when, at a secret signal during the service, everyone got up and started shaking hands all around the room. It was a friendly spirit, but I glanced over at Dede, and the bewildered expression on her face convinced me we should keep looking.

The following week we attended an Evangelical Free Church, and for the first time felt we might belong. The minister believed and preached the Bible. This made an impact on me, for I had been reading the Bible daily for the last year. In fact, on several occasions I had opened the Bible and had Scripture verses almost leap out at me as answers to my prayers. Dede said she enjoyed the services—as much as any pregnant woman can who has to hold a child on her lap —and we decided we would stick it out there. It was this minister who had come to call.

"You're kidding," one of my business associates said when I told him I was going to get out of business and enter the ministry. "What for?"

"I don't know," I answered. "I just have a feeling I should do something good for mankind."

"You mean you're going to become a priest or something?" he said unbelieving. "What about your booze? Your salty language? And those cigars?"

"I didn't say I was going to resign from the human race." I grinned. "But somebody's got to help this world out of the mess it's in, and I don't see where I'm making much of a contribution peddling electronic devices."

There were problems. Every dime we had was invested in the business. For me to pull out would mean the business would collapse, leaving my friends as broke as I would be. I knew this situation would have to be solved before I could do anything, yet I didn't see how. Well, as soon as I got my business and financial matters squared away, I would enter the ministry.

A month later, in early April 1956, I went home to Lexington to tell my mother of my decision.

I was sitting at the kitchen table while she prepared dinner, and her reaction came pretty much as a shock. "Pat, something's wrong. I don't think you have the slightest idea what you're talking about."

"But Mother, I thought this would be the thing that would please you most."

"It does please me, Son," she said, wiping her hands on a paper towel and sitting down across from me. "But how can you go into the ministry until you *know* Jesus Christ? You know how I know that you don't know him? Because you don't talk right. You never mention his name.

"You've got to accept him as Lord of your life, Pat. Unless you do, you're going to be just as spiritually empty a minister as you are a businessman. You cannot fill your emptiness by trying to do the work of God. It's like trying to fill a bottomless bucket. What you need is a new bucket. You need to be born again."

After dinner we sipped coffee as she repeated the same line I had heard since childhood: "The pulpits of our nation are filled with men just like you. They want to do good for mankind. They want to help people, but they're doing it in their own power, and that's worse than nothing. Jesus said, 'I am the way, the truth, and the life; no man cometh to the Father but by me.' There's no use going into the ministry, Pat, unless you've first surrendered your life to him."

I returned to New York the next day, still smarting under Mother's dogmatism. But deep in my inner spirit I felt that she was talking about something essential, something still hidden from me.

A week later I came in from work, and Dede handed me a note. "You got a phone call from this man in Philadelphia. He wants you to call him back."

I glanced at the note and saw the name: Cornelius Vanderbreggen. It was a name that was to change my life.

II

From Swinger to Saint

"You are the Lord's guest," the handsome Dutchman said as we looked at the menu in the elegant Philadelphia restaurant. "God is generous, not stingy. He wants you to have the best. Order anything you want."

I was impressed. Even though I had a sneaking suspicion that my mother had asked this missionary-evangelist to invite me to dinner, I could not escape his obvious sincerity. I was used to the expensive bistros around New York, but that a faith missionary should say the Lord had led him to dine at this resturant where the waiters wore white tie and tails was more than I could comprehend. I thought that God's people wore shabby clothes, baggy trousers, and suit coats that didn't match. I thought they ate hamburger and boiled turnips. But Cornelius Vanderbreggen certainly didn't fit that description.

Waiting to order, he began to talk easily about himself, allaying my suspicions with his charming but casual manner. He was a first generation American with a ministry in Holland as well as in Philadelphia. He talked excitedly about the Reapers' Fellowship in Gelderland and about Miracle Manor in Philadelphia. I identified with some of his experiences as a Marine Corps officer in World War II and felt a sense of relief sweeping over me, for somehow I had entertained ideas that this "evangelist" would put me on the spot by standing up in the middle of the dining room to lead in prayer. Swingers, you know, don't ever show themselves to be religious.

The headwaiter approached the table. Stiff. Dressed impeccably. Pencil poised over his order pad. I glanced back at my menu, and when I looked up I saw Vanderbreggen pulling a small pamphlet from his coat pocket and handing it to the waiter. "My name's Cornelius Vanderbreggen," he said warmly. "Here's a little booklet I've written, and I want you to have it."

I couldn't believe my eyes. The man was handing the waiter a Gospel tract. I was mortified beyond expression and quickly shifted my eyes back to the menu again.

Glancing back at the waiter, I saw him standing there, his face set like granite. My image as a swinger was rapidly dissolving. It took all the self-control I could muster to keep from groaning as I placed my order.

Beads of perspiration were popping out on my forehead as the protection of the menu was removed and I was once again face to face with this strange man. What had I gotten into? Was my mother to blame for this? I had never had any real contact with "religious" people who did crazy things like handing out tracts in restaurants. What next?

I didn't have to wait long to find out. Vanderbreggen, with no apparent awareness of my embarrassment and mortification, reached into his expensive briefcase beside the table and pulled out the biggest, blackest Bible I had ever seen.

"You know, Pat, this afternoon I was reading the Word and ran across an extremely interesting passage. Let me share it with you."

He pushed back the silver and the water glasses, and laying the huge Bible on the table, began to read out loud. I knew I had no choice but to sit there and act like I was listening. I could feel the moisture in the palms of my hands now, and little rivulets of perspiration running down my face. I tried to smile, but sensed my mouth had the shape of a crooked stick. I could feel a hundred pairs of eyes staring at us from all over the room while Vanderbreggen continued to read in a soft voice, accenting his thoughts with occasional gestures.

I tried to speak. "Mr. Vanderbreggen, you know I'm a Southern Baptist and . . ." I didn't get to finish. I saw the waiter coming. With quick strides he was advancing toward us, a dark scowl on his face. I knew we were about to be humiliated and asked to leave the restaurant. I kept wishing there were some way I could disappear under the table.

And then he was upon us. He cleared his throat. "Ahem . . ." Vanderbreggen hadn't seen him, or else had chosen to ignore him. He continued reading aloud from the Bible.

"Ahem." The waiter cleared his throat again. "Sir?"

Vanderbreggen looked up innocently.

"Sir, there is a lady over at the other table who is wondering what you are discussing."

I knew it. I dropped my head in my hands. Here it comes.

The waiter continued in his starched voice. "I gave her the little booklet you gave me. Can you give me another one?"

Had I heard correctly? I looked up as Vanderbreggen reached into his pocket and handed the waiter another tract. "Certainly, brother." He smiled. "By the way, have you ever had a personal experience with Jesus Christ?"

This isn't really happening, I thought.

"No sir," the waiter said, his eyes seeking the face of my host. "But recently I've been praying that God would help my friend in the hospital. Would this experience help me get through to God?"

I was aghast. Right here in the middle of this plush restaurant these two men were carrying on a conversation about Jesus Christ!

"Of course it would. Jesus said, 'No man cometh to the Father but by me.' "

There it was again—the same verse my mother had quoted. Vanderbreggen gave the waiter his card and invited him to call him. The waiter thanked him and marched stiffly back to his post.

I don't know the outcome of that encounter, but I do know that while Vanderbreggen was speaking to the waiter, something was happening to me. Suddenly I found myself sharing some of the deep things in my heart.

"During the past year I've been reading the Bible. Actually I've been devouring it. At times I think God has talked to me from it."

I paused, waiting to see how my host would react to such a radical idea. He just smiled.

I continued. "I'm convinced God is the only hope for this world."

I paused again, waiting for a reaction. Cornelius just nodded his head in agreement.

"In fact," I blurted out, "I've decided to enter the ministry. My only problem is how to get out of business without losing everything I've got."

Vanderbreggen totally ignored my "problem" and asked, "What do you believe about God?"

I felt my nervousness return and reached for a roll. "I believe he is the source of all power, the guiding intellect of the universe. Not only that, but I believe he has a destiny for each man's life, and that none of us will ever be happy or productive unless we are in the center of his will."

I had said it. I buttered my roll, expecting his word of approval.

"Pat, any Mohammedan could have told me what you just said. Isn't there something more?"

Suddenly I was oblivious to the surroundings. "Yes, there is something else. I believe Jesus Christ died for the sins of the whole world." I hesitated. I knew what he wanted, but I had never been willing to say it before. Now, to my amazement, I heard myself continue, ". . . and for my sins, too."

As soon as I said it, I looked up at my host. A slight smile was playing over his tanned face. A Bible verse I had learned flooded my consciousness. "If thou shalt confess with *thy mouth* the Lord Jesus . . . thou shalt be saved."

I knew I had been resisting that moment. Several times I had wanted to say it out loud, but never had been able to. Now the words had come from my mouth as well as from my heart, and no one could have been more amazed than I. Yet, even as I said the words, God turned on a light within me.

All my experiences with God so far had been religious—not spiritual. They had consisted of *my* search for him. Now I was beginning to understand his love for me, poured out through Jesus Christ. Every day for the last year I had prayed, "O Lord, in this life grant me the knowledge of thy truth and in the world to come life everlasting." Now suddenly, at this moment, God was answering both prayers.

It was as if I had walked through a curtain which had separated me from God. Suddenly I knew him, not just as God, but as Father. And I knew him because he had come to me in Jesus Christ.

I don't think Cornelius actually realized all that was taking place inside me at that moment. We continued our dinner and talked about many things, none of which I can remember. My mind was too caught up in the excitement of the fact that Jesus was God's Son— my Master!

After dinner (he paid the twenty-six-dollar bill and left a generous tip), we walked outside the restaurant and stood on the sidewalk across from the train station. The trees in the nearby park were just waking to spring, and a warm breeze fanned my face.

Cornelius reached up and laid his hand on my shoulder. "Pat, let's pray before you catch your train." He said it as though it were the most natural thing in the world for two grown men to stand in the middle of a Philadelphia sidewalk and pray. But no longer was I embarrassed. No longer did I worry about the people who had to walk around us as we stood with our heads bowed. No longer did I remember I was the son of a Senator. Now I was the son of the King. My heart filled with joy at the thought of it.

Cornelius shook my hand and quoted from Proverbs (3:5,6), a Scripture that was to be the guiding principle for my life from that moment on. "Trust in the Lord with all thine heart; and lean not unto thine own understanding. In all thy ways acknowledge him, and he shall direct thy paths."

"God wants you," Cornelius said, "to walk by faith and not by sight. If you lean on your own understanding, or depend on man's ways, you will miss the greatest joy—walking hand in hand with God, doing together the thing he has in mind."

I awoke the next morning with a tremendous urge to blaspheme God. Even though my vocabulary had become spiced with vulgarity, I never had actually taken the Lord's name in vain. Now, spontaneously, the actual words of blasphemy were coming to my lips.

I knew it was wrong. Turning over in bed I buried my face in my pillow and prayed. "God . . . I believe in you. Jesus, take this thing from me!"

Suddenly the desire was gone. Not only that, but as the day progressed I realized that something else was gone—my entire filthy vocabulary! I was a new person, in the words of Paul, "a new creation."

About three o'clock, sitting at my desk in my office, I leaned back in my chair and burst out laughing. I had been saved. I had passed from death into life. I was suddenly aware that I was living in an entirely new world. It was an indescribable sensation of joy and peace.

The hands of the clock moved to the familiar cocktail hour when all Manhattan stops working and starts drinking. Bill, my partner, appeared in the door of my office and said, "Let's go. Time to live."

"Bill, I am living—for the first time!" He gave me a strange look and went on out the door. I had no desire to go into those softly lit, upholstered sewers any longer. I had found a new kind of life. Real life. I could hardly contain my joy. I wanted to shout, and when I threw open the door of our living room, I did.

"Dede, I'm saved! *Saved!*" I grabbed her to me, lifting her off the floor.

Dede gave me a startled look and extricated herself. "Pat, you're drunk! Both of us are going to have to start cutting down on our drinking."

I began laughing. "Dede, I'm not drunk. I've been saved. I've met Jesus!"

"You met *who?*" She edged around the corner of the room and back into the kitchen. "Um, I'll have dinner ready in just a few minutes."

I followed her into the kitchen and squeezed her waist from behind as she stood at the stove. "I know I'm acting crazy. But honestly, something has happened to me. I've accepted Jesus Christ as my Savior."

Dede looked back over her shoulder, putting her face close to mine as she sniffed my breath. "You *have* been drinking, haven't you?" She said it almost hopefully.

I grinned. "I told you I hadn't. It's just that I'm saved. I know Jesus."

Breaking away from my embrace and wiping her hands on her apron, Dede set the casserole dish on the table and turned to look at me. "Pat, I believe in Jesus, too, but I don't go around shouting like a fanatic. And while we're talking about it, did you take the picture off the wall? I found it outside by the trash can."

"That's what I've been trying to tell you, honey," I said. "I'm a new man. No more of that old stuff."

Dede picked up Tim and put him in the high chair beside the table. Wiping a loose strand of hair from her eyes, she sat down. "Pat, I'm a Christian too."

"So was I—but now something's happened to me, and I want it to happen to you."

"I don't understand you," she said, frowning. "All my life I've believed in Jesus. He's always been there. In the Church, the Mass, the confessional. I don't need anything more to happen to me."

"But Dede, I know you, and you really do." I got up from the table and went into the living room, returning with my Bible. "Let me read you a couple of verses that explain what I'm talking about."

"Pat, you're being a fanatic!" Dede shouted. She pushed back from the table and ran into the other room. Tim, upset by the confusion, began to cry, and when I reached for him I turned over his milk.

"I don't care," I said to Timmy, or God, or whoever was listening. "Something tremendous has happened to me!"

By bedtime Dede had calmed down, and we were able to talk some more. Tim was asleep upstairs. Dede came back down and walked into the kitchen. I had finished putting up the dishes and was standing looking in the cupboard.

Dede stood in the door, watching. "Now what?" she asked, sarcastically.

I didn't say a word. I just reached up in the cabinet and began taking down the bottles of whiskey we had stored there. One by one I uncapped them and began pouring the whiskey down the sink. Glub . . . glub . . . glub . . .

"Have you completely lost your mind?" I heard Dede gasp. "That stuff costs money. What are you doing?"

"Sweetheart, I've got to do it," I said, watching the liquor swirl down the drain. "I'm not going to drink anymore."

"Well, maybe *you* are not going to drink anymore, but I feel like I need a good stiff one right now, the way you're acting. Just because you've lost your mind and become a religious nut doesn't mean I have to go crazy too."

She darted across the room and tried to grab the last bottle from the counter. I beat her to it, twisted the top off, and began pouring.

"Pat, be reasonable," she pleaded. "We paid good money for that. Let me have it."

She grabbed, but I held her off, pushing her away until the bottle was empty. She just stood silently, staring at the drain.

"Why, Pat, why?" She was sobbing softly.

I wanted to comfort her but didn't know what to say.

"Please trust me," I pleaded.

"But there's nothing wrong with drinking."

"There is for me, Dede. It represents my whole life apart from God."

"But what about me?" Dede exploded. "Do you expect me to sit around this house all day and take care of the baby and then listen to you read the Bible when you come home from wherever you've been? I don't mind you going into the ministry, but all this 'saved' stuff is too much for me. If you think I'm going to put up with this the rest of my life, you've got another think coming. I'll go back to Ohio. I want my children to grow up in a normal home."

Was she threatening divorce? I partially understood her turmoil. She had never known Jesus except as a remote, mystical object of veneration. Now that he had become alive and real to me, it scared her.

That night I began something else that was to take several weeks, and was to make a profound impact on my spiritual life. While Dede turned her back on the sofa bed and went to sleep, I sat at the little desk and began making a list of everyone I had ever wronged. It was a long list, and I realized that there were probably many names I couldn't remember. But I knew I needed to make restitution, so I began writing letters, asking the people to forgive me.

The first name on the list was the United States Marine Corps. While in service I was transferred from Quantico, Virginia, to Camp Pendleton, California. I had hitched a ride on a military transport plane, telling them I was on Marine Corps business. Then I had turned in a voucher for travel expenses as well. I explained the best I could what had happened to me and enclosed a check to reimburse the Marines for the $165 overpayment. Eventually they sent a curt acknowledgment. For all I know, my belated honesty may have upset the entire military budget.

I also began devouring my Bible, morning, noon, and night. I read it at meals. I read it aloud to Dede after we went to bed. Often she just turned over and went to sleep, but I read until I couldn't see anymore. As I read, one thing became clear to me: if I belonged to Jesus, so did my problems—even my business problems. So now I brought them to him.

Three of us, all members of the same class at Yale Law School, had invested money in a business that was producing electronic components. We had borrowed $6,000 (my share was $2,000) to produce a collapsible electronic speaker. I didn't have the money to pay off my share, and to walk out wouldn't be fair to my partners, so I prayed. "Lord, you've got to help me. I've given myself to you, and now I'm counting on you."

It was a crude prayer, but I was doing all I knew to do—trusting in the promises of God.

I didn't know when I prayed that prayer, that on that very day God was forging the last link in a chain of events that would solve my problem. A businessman in Seattle, Washington, an ungodly, profane man, just happened to come home from work that same evening and pick up his wife's Bible. The Bible fell open to Psalm 150 and the word "organ" caught his eye.

Since this man represented a church organ company, he read the verse. "Praise him with stringed instruments and organs." He read on. "Praise him upon the loud cymbals: praise him upon the high sounding cymbals."

The man stopped reading, remembering. A few days before, he had received an ad from our firm advertising that our speakers were especially good on high notes. The company he represented needed some kind of small electronic speaker that had good fidelity on high notes. The two things fitted together. He closed the Bible and called his travel agent.

The next day the man caught a plane in Seattle, picked up an associate in Cincinnati, and flew into New York. By the end of the day, we had sold him 25 percent of our business.

I was off the hook. I could leave clean. I didn't know where I was going, but I knew that in the fall I would be enrolled, someplace, in a seminary, preparing to become a minister for Jesus Christ.

III

Campus in the Woods

———
———
———

Dede was sitting at the breakfast table, her face streaked with tears. "Please, Pat, consider someone besides yourself."

I pushed my fork through the uneaten scrambled eggs growing cold on my plate. I knew it was hard on Dede. I had seen my mother suffer when Daddy had left on long trips or decided not to come home from Washington for weeks at a time. But Mother had adjusted, and so could Dede.

"Dede," I said, groping for words, "it's just something I've got to do."

"You're doing it because that Dutchman suggested it!" Dede exclaimed, her auburn hair still tousled from a sleepless night. "He got you 'saved,' and now he has suggested you go off in the woods to commune with God, and away you go."

"That's not fair," I argued. "Cornelius suggested it, but I'm going because Christ . . ."

"Pat, I've tried to adjust to this 'saved' jag you're on, but you've become a fanatic. All you do is read that Bible all day and sit around and talk to Jesus. I'm a nurse. I recognize schizoid tendencies when I see them, and I think you're sick. It's just not normal for a man to walk out on his wife and leave her with a small child when she's expecting a baby any minute—while he goes off into the woods to talk to God. God doesn't tell people to do things like that. At least, my God doesn't."

[18]

"He would if you really knew him—and you won't know him until you meet Jesus Christ."

"There you go again!" she said, pushing against the table and turning her chair away from me. "I feel like the whole world is coming apart around me. You've gone insane, Pat, and you're bent on taking me with you."

I got up and walked around to where she was sitting awkwardly in the chair. Her stomach, filled with child, covered her lap and kept her from bending over. She just sat there, her head down, her chin resting against her chest, the tears welling up and splashing on the little apron that looked ridiculous as it tried to cover her extended stomach. She seemed so big, so bulky, as I knelt beside her and tried to put my arms around her. "I won't be gone long. It's just something I have to do."

She shook her head and the tears continued to stream.

"I know you're upset. I know the baby's putting pressure on you mentally and physically. But Dede, this is God who's commanding me. I don't have any choice. I just want you to believe in me, to trust me. I love you. I'm not walking out on you. I'll be back."

She turned and buried her head in my shoulder. I could feel the warm dampness of her tears soaking through my shirt. It was summer already, and the heat was building up early, yet I felt the warmth of his love surrounding us as she relaxed in my arms. I wanted to cry too—a part of me did, but another part was rejoicing. "Sorrowing, yet always rejoicing." So this is what Paul meant. "Dede, God has something wonderful just ahead for both of us. A oneness closer than anything we've ever had—even in our best moments together."

Campus in the Woods is the Inter-Varsity Fellowship summer camp located at Lake of Bays, Canada. I arrived on a Wednesday afternoon, and Friday morning received a letter from Dede.

"Please come back. I need you desperately."

I stood in my cabin for a long time, looking at the letter. Was this

God telling me to go home, or was it Satan? I knew that this was no feminine ploy. Dede was desperate. What I had done to her was unforgivable unless God was in it. What a time to leave! The baby was due in eight weeks. We were moving to a furnished house in two weeks. Money was low, and I would be gone for a whole month. "God, you told me to come here. Can't you take care of her better than I could?" I looked at the letter again. "I need you desperately."

I picked up my Bible and went out through the woods toward the shore of the lake. The soft wind whispered through the treetops as I walked across the thick carpet of pine needles. I prayed, "Oh God, tell me what to do. I'm so inexperienced in your ways. Lead me. Guide me."

I sat down on a rock and looked out over the shimmering lake. "God, give me a word," I prayed. I let my Bible fall open. There on the page before me was his answer. "But I would have you without carefulness. He that is unmarried careth for the things that belong to the Lord, how he may please the Lord: But he that is married careth for the things that are of the world, how he may please his wife" (I Cor. 7:32).

It was as if God were saying, "Put me ahead of your wife and I'll take care of your wife."

I returned to my cabin and wrote Dede a brief note telling her what had happened. I closed saying, "I can't leave. God will take care of you."

The camp was located on an island in the middle of the lake. Most of the campers were college students who belonged to Inter-Varsity Fellowship and took a week or a month to come to this rustic retreat in the Canadian woods for Bible study, recreation, and prayer. One afternoon a group of us were sitting on the grass near the lake when we became aware of the community resort hotel on the mainland, a quarter of a mile away. We had known it was there, but hadn't paid much attention to it. It was a tourist resort for older people, but there was a large group of teenagers who came up during the summer to work—waiting on tables, running errands, and doing yard work.

Someone in the group spoke up and said, "We've been sitting here talking about the need to reach others for Christ, and right across the lake is a big group of kids. Why don't we do something about them?"

That afternoon, members of our group took the launch and went across to the hotel. They sought out the proprietress and asked if we could come over Sunday afternoon to speak to the teenagers.

"We've got too much happening Sunday to let them off to attend a meeting," she said. "But Tuesday is a slack day, and you can have a meeting with them that afternoon if you like."

The report brought a sense of disappointment. "Lord," I prayed inside, "you may know more about teenagers than I do, but Tuesday doesn't seem like a very good time." The woman couldn't be persuaded to change her mind, however, so we put up little signs around the hotel saying, "Worship service in the lounge. 2:00 p.m. Tuesday."

On the way back to our island, one of the boys in the group said, "Those kids aren't going to want to come inside for a worship service on Tuesday. That's their day to get out. They play tennis, swim, go boating. We'll be lucky if half a dozen show up."

Tuesday came, and I prayed for rain. "Lord, it's just got to rain, because if it doesn't, those kids aren't going to come inside."

Our island was about twenty acres with a ridge down the middle. The administration building and dining hall sat on the ridge, and the cabins were located at the water's edge. At noon I walked up the steep hill to the dining hall. As I passed the cabins, I spoke to the wife of one of the counselors.

"Beautiful weather," she said, glancing at the bright blue sky.

"I'm praying for rain," I said matter-of-factly.

"Goodness, I hope you're prayers aren't answered," she said. "I've got to get my wash out this afternoon."

"Insensitive creature," I muttered to myself as I trudged on up the hill. "Here the souls of kids are at stake, and she wants her wash to dry." I looked again at the sky. It was bright blue without a trace of clouds.

After lunch I went back to my cabin, shook my head, and said, "God, where is the rain?"

I walked out of the cabin toward the boathouse where we were to embark for the resort. As I walked along I heard a strange shooshing sound in the tops of the trees. It was mysterious. There was not the slightest trace of a breeze. The air was still, motionless. It was as if everything had ceased to move for a moment. I stopped and listened. The shooshing sound in the top of the trees continued, although not a leaf moved.

I glanced back behind the island, and far out over the lake I saw a little black cloud in the sky. As I watched, I could see it moving, all by itself, like a child's balloon that had drifted skyward and was propelled along by mysterious air currents. It scudded across the sky, looking every bit as if it were late, rushing as fast as it could to catch up.

I walked on to the boathouse, keeping a sharp lookout over my shoulder. By the time I got there, the little cloud had caught up with me. It was filled with water. Overflowing. The cloud seemed to stop over the boathouse, and I ran inside with the other fellows who had come down for the meeting. The rain fell in torrents, and then it stopped. Fearful, I looked outside only to see that the little cloud was moving again, out over the lake toward the resort center.

We let out a whoop and piled into the boat. By the time we got out in the lake, the cloud was halfway across the water with rain just pouring out of it in a little circle on the water underneath. We followed along behind it in the open boat, completely dry.

The cloud reached the resort center and stopped. Once again the rain fell in torrents. As we approached in the boat we could see the teenagers scurrying up from the beach and docks, running pell-mell toward the shelter of the dining hall. By the time we reached the dock, the rain had almost stopped, with just enough drops falling to let the kids think that it could start again any moment. When we got to the dining hall, the cloud had disappeared, as if it had wrung itself out over the resort and then evaporated into the air. We opened the door and walked in. The place was literally jammed with kids. They were sitting on the floor, standing around the walls, sitting on tables and chairs—and it was Tuesday afternoon.

I was learning to trust God. The following Sunday, I had my first opportunity to preach. A remote country church needed a preacher for that very Sunday. I was chosen.

I took my text from Daniel and preached on "Weighed in the Balances and Found Wanting." It was a glorious experience, and I returned to the island flushed with victory. And it was just at that time, about three Sunday afternoon, that Satan appeared to me.

I was in my cabin, lying on my cot, pondering the experiences of the morning when I heard Satan say, "Jesus is just playing you for a sucker, Robertson. You have already committed the unpardonable sin. Remember back in college when you told a joke and mentioned the Holy Spirit? That's the unpardonable sin. It says right in the Bible that God will never forgive anyone who does that. You can't be saved. You're hopeless. All this is just a cruel joke since you're bound for hell anyway."

I felt myself shaking, wavering. What Satan was putting in my mind was logical, and appealed to my legal reasoning. I had, indeed, told the joke. It happened once, and once was enough. But then I remembered the words of those young boys in Daniel who told the king that even if God didn't deliver them from the fiery furnace they would still not blaspheme him. I said, "Devil, it may be. But I still know that Jesus is my Savior. Even in hell I'll praise him."

"The pangs of hell got hold upon me," the psalmist had cried, and that afternoon I experienced them for myself. It was terrible—and as real as anything I'd ever known. A dark roll of despair was trying to envelop me. By the end of the afternoon I had won, but I was physically and spiritually drained. It took days to completely recover.

I didn't understand what was happening at Campus in the Woods, but daily I became aware of this strange and mysterious presence of the Holy Spirit that surrounded the island. Cornelius was there, teaching every day, and I was feasting on his teaching and drinking in his wisdom from the Bible. Whenever he came in, I would go up to him and begin asking questions, hanging on every word he said.

Then one night he did the strangest thing. It was almost midnight, and several of us were sitting around the room talking. Unexpectedly, Cornelius rose to his feet and said, "God has just told me to go west."

"Where are you going?" someone asked.

"I don't know," the handsome Dutchman said as he headed to his room to begin packing. "But I have learned that when God speaks I must follow. All I know is that I'm supposed to go west."

Within the hour he was gone, catching the launch to the mainland where his car was parked and then off into the middle of the night. Little did I know this would be the last time I would see him. But this one thing I did know—God had removed my teacher because he wanted me to look only to him. He wanted me to mature quickly because he had work for me to do.

It was the first of August when I returned to New York. The heat rose in shimmering waves from the streets as I got off the train and caught a cab to our house on Staten Island. I arrived in time to learn from a neighbor that Dede had just rushed our twenty-month-old son, Tim, to the hospital. He had apparently eaten Saniflush. This was bad enough for Timmy, but what would it do to Dede—only two weeks from giving birth to our second child? I had every reason to panic, but all I felt was peace. It was amazing. I knew God was going to keep his promise to me.

Dede arrived a few moments later, the picture of calm, and when we got back to the hospital, what a sight awaited us! There sat Timmy, tears streaming down his cheeks while two chubby hands pushed turkey into his mouth. Just then the doctor appeared. "We can't find anything wrong with him, Mr. Robertson," he said, and then he chuckled. "You'd better get him out of here before we have to charge you double board."

The next ten days were really great! Dede was so glad to have me back that she put out of her mind the fact that I did not have a job or any immediate prospects of one. We were going to be parents again, and God allowed us a time to enjoy one another. I held a volunteer position at *Faith at Work* magazine in New York. It occupied my time, but paid nothing. Big decisions faced me, but I was content to await God's next move in them.

Then Dede's mother arrived. She had come to be with us when the baby was born.

She never had liked me, having felt that Dede should have married a Catholic—a wealthy one. Quite understandably, my recent actions had only reinforced her opinion that I was an irresponsible, selfish brute who was more interested in myself than in her precious daughter. She blew in from overseas like a squall line approaching the shore. The first flurry struck at dinner that night.

"How do you expect to support two children?" she queried. "Dede tells me you've gone to work for a religious magazine. You can't make enough that way to support a family."

I dreaded telling her what kind of job it actually was, but she wrung it out of me.

"Well, are you going to tell me, or aren't you? How much does it pay? What are the retirement benefits?"

"Well, it's just temporary until I go to the seminary in the fall. I volunteered my services and . . ."

"I don't believe it!" she said, her eyes flashing. "You *volunteered* your services? A Phi Beta Kappa with a law degree volunteering his services to a religious magazine? You mean, you're working for nothing?"

"Well, it's not that I don't want to work for money," I said. "It's just that God has told me to—"

"Don't tell me about God! I'm a lot older than you, and I've belonged to the church all my life. I could teach you a thing or two

about God, but I don't think you'd listen. I don't care if you are the
son of a Senator, I think you've turned into some kind of religious
oddball, and if Dede had any sense, she'd come home with me and
leave you for good. Imagine! A man with two children and two degrees working for nothing! It's ridiculous!"

Elizabeth was born August 14, 1956, and after Dede returned
from the hospital, I made an earnest effort to spend time praying
with her about God's plan for our lives. At least I prayed, while she
listened. The immediate question was how and where did he want
me to prepare for the ministry.

A friend had recommended Gordon Divinity School a few miles
outside of Boston. They had living quarters available, and we were
having to give up our Staten Island home anyway. So one evening I
sat down and wrote a letter to Gordon.

"Dear Sirs: I want to apply for admission to your school, for I feel
it is the Lord's will . . ."

I got that far and stopped. I turned to Dede who was sitting on the
sofa feeding the baby. "I don't feel any such thing."

"Don't feel what?" she asked.

"I don't feel it is God's will for me to go to Gordon."

"Oh, Pat, you mean we have to go through *that* all over again? I
just don't know whether I can take it. Can't you ever make up your
mind about anything?"

I crossed the room and sat down beside her. "Every time I make
up my mind, God changes it. Maybe if I would let him control it
from the beginning, I wouldn't have to do all this starting and stop-
ping." I picked up my Bible and put it in my lap. "God, what do you
want me to do?" I prayed.

I opened the Bible and reached out and put my finger in the middle of one of the pages. I read the verse I was pointing at: "Say not
ye, There are yet four months, and then cometh harvest? behold, I
say unto you, Lift up your eyes, and look on the fields; for they are
white already to harvest" (John 4:35).

"You see," I almost shouted to Dede who was sitting there dumbfounded. "God doesn't want me to go all the way up to Gordon—he wants me to stay here."

"How in the world can you get that out of what you just read?"

"Gordon is 250 miles away, and it's in the country. But see, it says here the fields are at hand, and the harvest is right here—all around me. He wants me to stay in New York."

Dede's eyes filled with tears, and she hugged the tiny infant in her arms close to her breast. "Pat, please. I'll try to adjust to almost anything, but I can't stand this uncertainty."

I knew God had spoken. I walked back to the typewriter, pulled the paper from the carriage and tore it up. "I'm going to give the Lord time to provide for us," I said. "He will show me where he wants me to go . . ." But I was talking to the walls. Dede had left the room, crying.

"Biblical Seminary is a downtown school in Manhattan with a three-year course of inductive Bible study," one of the fellows at *Faith at Work* said. "Why don't you check it out?"

That afternoon I rode over to East 49th Street to look at the facilities and talk to the dean. The seminary was housed in a twelve-story building at 235 East 49th Street, which included dorm space for single students, classrooms, library, and administrative offices. It was fully accredited, and the inductive course of study would make it possible for me to take whatever subjects appealed to me most. I returned to the house and assured Dede that this was the place God wanted me to go.

However, there were still problems involved, not the least of them being the fact that we were going to have to move from our house. Without funds it was going to be difficult to find a place to live near the school. Once again we were going to have to walk by faith.

I began to ask around, and we finally found an apartment in Far Rockaway which rented for $125 per month. This was more than we could afford, but it was the cheapest we'd found. Far Rockaway was the jumping-off-place into nowhere; it was going to take half my time

going and coming from school, and Dede would be even more secluded than she had been on Staten Island.

The day I was to sign the lease, I received a phone call from one of
the housing administrators I knew in Queens. He had worked for my
father in Washington, and I had asked him to be on the lookout for
an apartment. Since I had not heard from him, I had concluded he
had forgotten about me. "You must really have been on your knees,"
he said when he called.

"What do you mean?"

"I mean I've found an apartment for you. It's an elevator apartment with two bedrooms in Queens at the Lord Ashley. The rent is
fifty-six dollars per month."

"I can't believe it," I said, having difficulty holding still.

"That's not all. It has wall-to-wall carpeting, and the rent includes
both water and electricity. Like I said, man, you must have been on
your knees."

"When is it available?"

"Right now." I was remembering Cornelius Vanderbreggen's
statement, "God is generous, not stingy. He giveth us all things richly
to enjoy."

I didn't realize it at the time, but the apartment was an equal distance, almost to the block, from Biblical Seminary in one direction
and the Bayside Community Methodist Church in the other. And
three weeks later, when I enrolled at the seminary, I understood why
God had put us exactly there. Each student was to be assigned work
in a local church in some kind of staff position. I was assigned to
work as a student assistant pastor—at the Bayside Community Methodist Church.

IV

A Quest for Power

My first year at Biblical Seminary was a time of fulfilment and frustration. For the first time in my life I felt satisfied, knowing I was in the will of God. However, as I studied the Scriptures, I felt a growing frustration; the accounts of the miracles of Jesus and the disciples in the Gospels and in the Book of Acts confused me. "Jesus is the same yesterday, today, and forever," the professors said. Yet I saw no modern-day evidence of healings or deliverance from demons or the other miracles he performed. I wasn't sure what that meant, but I was sure we weren't experiencing it. In my frustration I began to cry out to God for the answer.

One by one I came into contact with other students who felt the same way. One was a young Presbyterian minister named Dick Simmons. Dick and his wife Barbara had graduated from seminary in San Francisco and gone to Tucson, Arizona, for his first pastorate. He had flopped. Desperately mixed up, he kept remembering a life-changing experience he had had with the Holy Spirit during the 1951 Billy Graham crusade in Seattle, and he longed for it to return to his life. He had resigned his church in Tucson, sold all their belongings, put their clothes in a duffel bag and caught a bus to New York to enroll at Biblical Seminary. Unless, he said, he found the reality of the Holy Spirit that he had once known, he was going to quit the ministry.

Another student was Dick White. Dick had been a staff member of Inter-Varsity Fellowship at Columbia University. Shortly after school began, he asked Dick Simmons to speak at an IVF Conference. Simmons refused, saying, "I'd like to, but frankly, I'm a cheap hypocrite. I've experienced things with God, but I'm not walking in them now, and I can't see playing the role of a hypocrite any longer."

This kind of blunt honesty really jolted Dick White, and he wound up joining several of us in a prayer group that was meeting daily.

Others in the group were Lois Ostensen, who later became Dr. Ockenga's assistant at Park Street Church in Boston, and Gene Peterson, ex-Pentecostal turned Presbyterian, who was the president of the student body. Gene later pastored the Presbyterian Church at White Plains, New York.

We began meeting at 6:30 A.M. in one of the dormitory rooms. As we talked and prayed, it became obvious we were all seeking the same thing: revival. We wanted it in our personal lives and in the life of the seminary.

One morning Dick White came to the meeting aglow. "I have just finished reading the most fantastic report I've ever seen," he said. "It is an account of what has been happening in the Hebrides Islands off the north shore of Scotland. Duncan Campbell has been touring the U.S. and Canada sharing what is happening. Revival has broken out in the Hebrides."

All of us caught Dick's excitement and plied him with questions. "The whole chain of islands has been ripped by the power of God," Dick continued. "Ten years ago a group of Christians took a census and said they couldn't find one man under thirty in any of the churches. Alarmed by this report, they got together and said they would make a solemn covenant that they would not rest or cease from prayer until God visited the islands with revival."

"Wow! That's some kind of prayer," Gene Peterson said softly.

"According to the report shared by Campbell," Dick continued, "these men and women waited through the nights before peat fires, pleading one promise, 'I will pour water upon him that is thirsty and floods upon the dry ground.' They declared that promise was made by a covenant-keeping God who must be true to his covenant engagements. Months passed, and then Mr. Campbell joined the group. One night at a farmhouse they spent the entire night in prayer. About one o'clock Campbell asked a young man to pray. He rose to his feet and prayed, 'Lord, you made a promise. Are you going to fulfill it? We believe that you are a covenant-keeping God. Will you be true to your covenant? You have said you would pour water on the thirsty and floods upon the dry ground. I do not know how others stand in your presence. I do not know how the ministers stand. But if I know my own heart, I know where I stand, and I tell thee now that I am thirsty.' Then he said this: 'Lord, before I sit down, I want to tell you that your honor is at stake.' "

We had never heard of anyone praying like that. "What happened?" I asked.

"Campbell testifies that as the man sat down the house began to shake like a leaf. The dishes rattled on the sideboard, and the people were terrified. Campbell pronounced the benediction, and the Christians hurried out into the streets of the village only to find them filled with people; all of them were hurrying toward the little church carrying stools and chairs and asking, 'Is there room for us in the church?' "

We sat in silence as Dick finished his report. I could feel the hair on the back of my neck standing on end and felt goosebumps rising on my skin. This was real. This was what we had been longing to hear about.

"That happened ten years ago," Dick said. "Just recently they took another census in the islands and couldn't find a young man under thirty who *wasn't* a believer—a complete reversal."

It was difficult to grasp that such a thing could actually happen in the twentieth century. It sounded like Pentecost repeated.

"Did the revival actually start through Duncan Campbell?" I asked.

"He says not," Dick said, referring to a report in his hand. "It seemed to spring up spontaneously all over the islands. In one church, the people were waiting before God and nothing happened, until a teenage girl stood to her feet and said, 'I love Jesus with all my heart.' The people began to weep, and they stayed until three in the morning, confessing their sins and worshiping the Lord."

After hearing this fantastic account of the outpouring of the Holy Spirit, we all sat in silence. Then Dick Simmons spoke up: "Without revival, there's nothing. There's no hope."

We agreed and decided that from that time on we would meet daily to ask God to pour out his Spirit in our lives and on the seminary.

One morning as we met to pray, Dick Simmons told the group that we weren't the only ones in the seminary on this quest for power. "There is a Korean woman named Su Nae Chu, who goes up to the upper room on the twelfth floor of the seminary every morning at this same hour to pray."

"Why don't we get together?" I asked.

Little did we suspect what a profound influence this diminutive Korean woman was going to have on our lives.

Su Nae Chu was in her late thirties, the widow of a well-known Presbyterian pastor who had been martyred during the Korean War. She had come to New York to do graduate work at the seminary and was planning to go back to Korea to teach in a Bible college.

Revival, she told us, had also broken out in Korea. In fact, she had been in the middle of it. She had been the "mother" of a school for beggar boys in Korea. These kids, who made their living stealing from garbage cans on the streets, were like animals. Even after they were confined in the orphanage, they stole from each other. After failing to see any improvement in them, Su Nae decided to fast and pray for revival to break out in the orphans' home. "I shall not eat until the power of God falls on you," she told the rebellious children.

They laughed at her, saying she would sneak around and steal food just like them. "No," she said. "I am going to lock myself in my room without food. There I shall remain, praying, until your lives are changed by the power of God."

Su Nae Chu had gone to her room and locked the door. She remained there several days, spending most of the time on her knees on a small mat in the middle of the room. The children grew concerned and peeked through the keyhole and saw her on her knees, praying.

Suddenly God poured out his Spirit upon the whole orphanage. These kids, who had been at each other's throats and stealing food, were now stumbling all over themselves trying to serve each other. They ended up putting blankets over their shoulders and going out at five in the morning to pray in the peach orchard. Then they went down into the community to make restitution—asking the villagers to forgive them.

This confirmed what we had heard about the Hebrides. Here was a woman in our own midst who had seen revival and testified that through fasting and prayer the lives of children were changed without a word having been spoken.

"The secret to such prayer," said Su Nae, "is praying in tongues."

Immediately I was intrigued and began to quiz Su Nae about her experiences.

"They used to call me the 'tongues woman' in Korea," she said. "After revival came, I got up every morning and went up into the hills and walked around the mountain praying in tongues.

"But you must seek the Holy Spirit, not tongues," Su Nae cautioned. "Ask Jesus to baptize you in his Spirit, and then you may claim all the manifestations of the Spirit—including tongues."

So we began praying for the baptism in the Holy Spirit, not only for ourselves, but for the seminary. Day after day we met to kneel or prostrate ourselves on the floor to weep, and to pray. Su Nae Chu became the prayer strength of our school. She would pray, crying and travailing in the Spirit for many hours at a time, saying, "O Lord, so proud . . . so proud . . . so proud."

The morning prayer meetings were extended to the noon hour, and finally we began to meet at night, gathering in the dormitory rooms, going to various churches about the city where the power of Pentecost was preached, or meeting in each other's apartments. We now had proof of revival not only in New Testament times, but in our own generation as well. The big question remained: Could it come to America also?

V

Drunk on New Wine

Exciting things began to happen in the spring of 1957. All of us in the prayer group, which now included Dede, had volunteered to serve as counselors for the Billy Graham crusade scheduled to open in Madison Square Garden on May 15.

The week before the crusade was to begin, word leaked out that the Holy Spirit had fallen on the Graham team. Leighton Ford, Graham's brother-in-law, had led a devotional retreat for the team at Wainwright House at Rye, New York, on Long Island Sound. As he gave a challenging, convicting message, all of the team, including Graham himself, were broken by the Holy Spirit. They ended on their knees in repentance and tears. The next day, Scotchman Ralph Mitchell spoke, and it happened all over again. "God has filled us with his Holy Spirit," Graham was quoted as saying.

Perhaps, just perhaps, revival will come to New York through Billy Graham, we thought. All of us began praying for the Holy Spirit to fall on the city during the Graham crusade. However, our own particular blessing was to come in an entirely different way.

Halfway through the crusade, Barbara Simmons, Dick's wife, boarded a bus one night to return home from one of the meetings at Madison Square Garden. As she got on, she noticed another woman on the bus wearing a counselor's badge. Barbara sat down beside her and introduced herself. The woman was a Mrs. Edwards from Los Angeles who followed Billy Graham at her own expense, to pray for revival.

This excited Barbara, since revival was the thing we had all been praying for. She invited the woman to come to her house the next night for dinner. The whole prayer group showed up and listened with rapt attention as Mrs. Edwards told her story.

Mrs. Edwards was a short, plump, cheerful little lady in her late sixties or early seventies. After dinner, she began to share the experiences her prayer group had in Los Angeles when Billy Graham held his first big meeting in 1949—the meeting which catapulted him into international fame.

Armin Gesswein, a Los Angeles Lutheran minister who had shared in the 1937 revival in Norway, had told Graham, "Whenever God is going to do any kind of work, He always begins by prayer." Grady Wilson had come early to Los Angeles to organize prayer chains and prayer bands. One of those prayer bands meeting nightly before and during the crusade was Mrs. Edwards' group, which ordinarily met to pray for Charles E. Fuller and the Old-Fashioned Revival Hour.

The night before the crusade began in the Canvas Cathedral at the corner of Washington Boulevard and Hill Street on the edge of the skyscraper district, Graham had heard about Mrs. Edwards' prayer group and asked if he might meet with them.

"Please pray for me," he said. "I'm just a country lad. All on the team are country lads, and we don't know how to handle these big meetings. Pray not only for souls to be won, but pray that revival may come."

Sensing that God had far more in store for Los Angeles than the thirty-year-old evangelist dreamed, this small prayer group covenanted together to meet every night to undergird the crusade in prayer.

"After three weeks the campaign was drawing to a close," Mrs. Edwards continued. "Although the tent had been filled each night, and hundreds had come to Christ, there was still no evidence of revival. Graham had announced he was praying whether to close the meeting or continue on. Therefore, we decided to meet and pray throughout the night, since he would have to announce his decision the following night."

As they knelt in prayer, they sensed the power of the Lord in the room. "It was as though the ceiling were about to fall," Mrs. Edwards said, her eyes shining as she remembered the excitement of that hour. "Every one of us in that room could feel an actual Presence hovering over our heads.

" 'What is it?' some of the ladies asked in fright. 'Is it the coming of Christ? Is it the judgment? Is it revival?' So great was the power of the Presence in the room that it was like a cloud of fire suspended over our heads.

"None of us knew what it was, but we were agreed on one thing: whatever it was, it was of God. 'Let's ask God to drop it on us, whatever it is,' I said.

"So we all pulled out our pillows (remember, we were old ladies and that floor was hard), and we knelt and began praying that God would let his Spirit fall, not only on us, but on Los Angeles. Oh, it was an exciting moment."

Mrs. Edwards paused, wiping tears from her eyes. The rest of us were so caught up in the excitement of the description we could hardly breathe. She continued.

"As we prayed, the phone in the room began ringing. One of the ladies answered, and it was Billy Graham. 'Are those women praying for me again? I'm here in my hotel room so filled with the Holy Spirit that I can't sleep. I've been pacing the floors, preaching to the walls and the furniture. I can't stop.'

"Everyone in the room began to praise God. We knew we were going to have a revival."

I glanced sideways at Dede. She was drinking in the testimony of this simple but profound woman. Mrs. Edwards shook her head slowly as if she still had trouble believing all that had taken place. "The next day one of the ladies called me, highly excited. 'Quick, turn on your radio and listen to Stuart Hamblen,' she said. Then she hung up.

"I never listened to Stuart Hamblen although he was one of the most popular men in Hollywood. I much preferred to listen to a good Christian program rather than his country western show when he talked about his drinking, gambling, and racehorses. However, I twisted the dial of my kitchen radio and heard Hamblen's voice coming through the speaker.

" 'Last night at two o'clock, after getting drunk earlier in the evening,' he was saying, 'I went to Billy Graham's hotel apartment. At five o'clock this morning I gave my heart to Jesus Christ. I've quit smoking, and I've quit drinking. I'm going to sell my racehorses and never race again. And tonight, at the end of Billy's invitation, I'm going to hit the sawdust trail.'

"I shouted, Hallelujah!" Mrs. Edwards beamed. "I knew revival was going to come. But there was more.

"Graham continued the meeting for one more week, and the crowds almost doubled in size. At the end of the week he said he was praying whether to close out the meeting or keep it going. That morning I was home alone, reading my Bible, and I heard a voice in my mind that said, 'Pick up your phone and call William Randolph Hearst.' Of course everyone in Los Angeles knew that Hearst was the publisher of the *Los Angeles Examiner* and the *Herald Express*, but I didn't understand why God was telling a person like me to call a man like that. I argued with God, but the voice was insistent. 'Call Hearst.'

"That afternoon I screwed up my courage, picked up the phone and dialed San Simeon, Hearst's fabled estate. When a servant answered I said simply, 'I would like to speak to William Randolph Hearst.' Moments later I heard his voice on the other end of the line, and at the same time I felt the anointing power of the Spirit of God descend just like it had the week before. I spoke with an eloquence I could never have generated myself as I told this hardnosed newspaperman about the Billy Graham revival and how I felt he was God's man for this nation. He listened, thanked me politely, and we hung up.

"That night, as we met before the crusade service, I shared what had happened. Those in my prayer group were agog. 'You mean you talked to Hearst personally? No one *ever* gets to talk to Hearst. You have to go through batteries of secretaries. It's easier to get hold of the President of the United States than to get hold of Hearst. How did you get through?'

"I just shrugged my shoulders and said, 'I picked up the phone and they put me right through. Just like that.'

"That night Billy arrived at the tent to find the place swarming with reporters and photographers. Flashbulbs exploded everywhere. Billy had to stop in the middle of his sermon to ask a man to climb down from a stepladder he had placed right in front of the platform. He was interviewed long into the night, and the next day the *Examiner* and the *Herald Express* carried banner headlines. Little did I know that as a result of that phone call William Randolph Hearst would send out a two-word endorsement to the Hearst chain that would catapult Billy Graham from his position as an obscure Youth for Christ evangelist into world fame, where he would become personal confidant of presidents and be acknowledged as the most famous Christian on the earth. For out of that phone call came Hearst's famous wire to all the papers in his chain: 'Puff Graham.' "

Mrs. Edwards was in tears again but went on. "The greatest thing that happened was that revival came to Los Angeles. It just came for a brief moment, but it came. All over the city, people were talking about Billy Graham—and about Jesus. The cabbies, the waitresses, and the shopgirls. Everyplace you went, you heard conversations about Jesus. Before each service, church people stood shoulder to shoulder, overflowing the prayer tent. The leader's desk was piled so high with written prayer requests that many could not be mentioned. The campaign extended from three weeks to eight, and more than four thousand found Jesus as personal Savior."

Mrs. Edwards finished talking and we sat quietly in the front room of Dick Simmons' house. All of us were lost in our thoughts. To me, this was further confirmation that God still pours out his Spirit when the conditions are right. First we had heard about the revival in the Hebrides. Then Su Nae Chu's experience in Korea. Now Mrs. Edwards' testimony which was, again, firsthand.

"Are we experiencing revival in New York?" I finally asked her.

"No," she said. "We are experiencing evangelism. But what we had in Los Angeles was revival."

"But what's the difference?" I wanted to know.

"Revival is a moving of God among his people, and an awareness of God laying hold of an entire community. In a successful evangelistic campaign, many are brought to a saving knowledge of the truth, and the church will be enlarged, but in revival the fear of God lays hold upon the community, moving men and women who until then had no concern for spiritual things, to seek after God. When revival comes, all the mechanics fall away, and the Spirit of God takes over, doing things men would never dream of. This is what I am praying for."

"Yes," someone murmured softly, "and this is what we are praying for, too."

It seemed that everyone I talked to, every book I read, concerned personal revival. A week later I picked up a book in the seminary library by evangelist Charles G. Finney. Since Finney, like myself, had started out as a lawyer, I took the book home to read. I could hardly believe it. Finney, like Su Nae Chu and others, had been baptized in the Holy Spirit and had apparently spoken in tongues. The passage concerning his baptism was so thrilling, I could not sleep for lying awake praising God for what had happened. Here's Finney's account.

"I returned to the front office, and found that the fire that I had made of large wood was nearly burned out. But as I turned and was about to take a seat by the fire, I received a mighty baptism of the Holy Ghost. Without any expectation of it, without ever having the thought in my mind that there was any such thing for me, without any recollection that I had ever heard the thing mentioned by any person in the world, the Holy Spirit descended upon me in a manner that seemed to go through me, body and soul. I could feel the impression, like a wave of electricity, going through and through me. Indeed, it seemed to come in waves and waves of liquid love; for I could not express it in any other way. It seemed like the very breath of God. I can recollect distinctly that it seemed to fan me, like immense wings.

"No words can express the wonderful love that was shed abroad in my heart. I wept aloud with joy and love; and I do not know but I should say, I literally bellowed out the unutterable gushings of my heart. These waves came over me, and over me, and over me, one after the other, until I recollect I cried out, 'I shall die if these waves continue to pass over me.' I said, 'Lord, I cannot bear anymore'; yet I had no fear of death."

Finney attributed his experience to a reckless quest for God. Su Nae Chu had fasted and prayed. The more I read of Finney's turning aside and seeking the face of the Lord, I realized this was what I should do also. The others in the prayer group agreed, and Dick Simmons, Gene Peterson, Dick White, and I decided to take three days off and find a quiet place away from the city where we could fast and pray.

A young Christian friend of mine, Al Thyberg, owned a rough campsite up near New Preston, Connecticut, where he took boys from the New York area for summer retreats. He had just purchased an abandoned farm adjoining the camp, and we asked if we could take our sleeping bags, drive up, and spend a few days seeking the face of the Lord in the empty farmhouse. He graciously consented.

The long-abandoned farmhouse had been built before the Revolutionary War. While we laid out our sleeping bags, Simmons wandered away to walk through the woods. Moments later he came tearing back, shouting, laughing, and praising God. He was beside himself with ecstasy, and all he could do was point out into the woods.

He fairly pulled us down a small path. Running through the underbrush, we suddenly came to a tiny clearing in the middle of which was a stone monument. I ran around to the front and read the inscription:

BIRTHPLACE OF CHARLES G. FINNEY
1792
Attorney, Evangelist, College President
Man of God

It was as though we were on holy ground, and we kicked off our shoes and began laughing and praising God. I knew the Holy Spirit had allowed us to come to this place for a sign. He was about to pour himself out on us even as he did on Finney.

Even though we did not receive the baptism in the Holy Spirit that weekend as we hoped, we did return with new spiritual sensitivity. I had been seeking to be filled with the Holy Spirit; now God showed me his emphasis. He is the *Holy* Spirit. He is the Spirit of Truth. He showed me that I was to despise all manner of lying and dishonesty. Before I could come into his presence, I first had to have clean hands and a pure heart. It was a magnificent revelation. He was saying to me, "I hate lying. I demand truth in your inward being." God had put his finger on a raw nerve. My southern upbringing had taught me always to be gracious, even at the expense of the truth. Later on, it grew increasingly easy to alter the truth to suit my convenience. Now, after the three-day fast, I had become so sensitive to the truth that I couldn't stand falsehood. When anyone made a misstatement of fact in my presence, I felt as if a knife had been twisted in my stomach. I believed that God had given me the key to the fullness of His power.

But no sooner had I returned to New York, than Satan dealt me a body blow. He struck Dede.

Dede had been pregnant, carrying what would have been our third child. Shortly after my return from the retreat, full of the glory of God and determined to become holy, Dede started to miscarry and was confined to bed. Overnight, I, the glorious seeker after God, was turned into a frayed housekeeper. I was suddenly faced with all the domestic chores in our apartment—cooking, cleaning, washing dishes, caring for the children—plus having to nurse my sick wife. It was nerve-shattering.

"Lord," I cried out, "I received a command from you to be holy, and now you are allowing Satan to dissipate my zeal through the pressures of stupid things like housework and cooking. I want to be out winning souls for Jesus' sake, but I am forced to stay home and take care of my wife and children. I want to fast and pray and seek more of you, and I am tied down to a sinkful of dirty dishes and a pailful of messy diapers. O God, it is enough." For me, it was too much.

Later I was to learn that this is one of God's ways of maturing his sons, and that I was just part of a great pattern. Even the prophet Elijah experienced glorious victory on Mt. Carmel one day only to find himself running for his life the next.

I was also beginning to realize that the devil hits the weakest member. Sometimes I would be getting ready to go to church where I was to preach or minister, and Dede would stalk into the room, making unkind remarks, and drain all my spiritual zeal in a matter of seconds. Lacking the full resources of the Holy Spirit, I would react, and before long my reaction was worse than her action. Then I would storm out of the house, acting far more like a minion of Satan than a son of God.

As Dede regained her health, I again started visiting other churches in the evening, seeking the baptism in the Holy Spirit. Dede's reactions to this were intense. "Every night you've been off having a hallelujah time with all your new friends, and I'm stuck here at home looking after the children. If you're seeking this baptism in the Holy Spirit that you talk about all the time, I think you can get it just as well in your own living room as you can in all these meetings."

Even though her words were spoken in anger, I sensed they had prophetic overtones.

During the summer of 1957, the prayer meetings became weekly occurrences in our home, but Dede always seemed to find some kind of excuse for getting up and leaving the room. I knew that unless there was a direct intervention from the Lord, the spiritual gap that was forming would soon be so wide it would be impossible to bridge. Yet I knew I had no alternative but to press on in the Spirit, despite her objections.

Toward the end of the summer, my mother suggested that we take a two-week vacation at her expense and go up to Jack Wyrtzen's Word of Life Camp on Scroon Lake. Dede was willing to do anything to get out of the city and away from those "weird people," as she called the folk who were continually coming to the house.

Word of Life Camp is located on an island in the middle of a cold-water lake nestled in the Adirondack Mountains in upper New York state. The camp had recently purchased a beautiful Inn on the mainland where we were to stay.

The second week we were there, I told Dede I would take care of the children so she could attend one of the evening services at the pavilion. Larry McGuill, a Baptist preacher from Wycoff, New Jersey, was to preach.

That night Larry preached on hardening one's heart until it can no longer respond to the voice of Jesus. Dede was deeply moved in her spirit as she sat listening at the rear of the huge auditorium. Yet, when the altar call was given, her pride surged to the surface, preventing her from leaving her seat. Realizing she was doing exactly what the preacher had been talking about, she began to weep. She felt crushed as if under a heavy weight. Softly, but in deep contrition, she cried, "Jesus, come into my life."

And he did. Suddenly she knew it. She had been reborn, and in that same moment the weight had lifted. She was not completely free, but Jesus had begun to strip away the cocoon that had held her imprisoned all these years.

It was late when she returned to the Inn. I didn't know that anything had happened, but an inner work had begun in her life. Several years were to elapse before I would know the full import of what had happened that night.

Returning to New York, I began my junior year of school. As my search for God intensified, I was becoming aware that one by one God was bringing across my path the men he had chosen to help me.

I was invited to the Presidential Prayer Breakfast in Washington, D.C., to speak to the Senate prayer group of which my father was a member. At the end of a meeting, Bob Walker, the ruggedly handsome editor of *Christian Life*, came over to me, chatted a bit, and then asked, "Have you ever heard of the baptism in the Holy Spirit?"

"That's the experience I have been searching for," I replied, but before I could finish my sentence, we were interrupted, leaving me wondering why he would ask me such a question.

I returned to New York, and arriving at Penn Station went directly to the annual banquet of Christian Soldiers, Inc., on whose board I was a member. Seated at the head table with me was an ebullient young minister, Harald Bredesen, who, it turned out, was public-relations director for the Gospel Association for the Blind. I was drawn to him by his warmth of spirit and was delighted when we discovered at the conclusion of the banquet that we were taking the same subway home. We were no sooner seated than with an engaging smile he asked, "Do you know anything about the baptism in the Holy Spirit?"

"Funny you should ask," I replied. "Just today in Washington I met a fellow named Bob Walker, and he asked me the same question."

"Bob Walker!" he exclaimed. "He's one of my best friends. He's just received the baptism. That's why he wanted to share it with you." Harald was exuberant—I was awed by the providence of God.

It was time to leave, and as the doors of the car swished shut behind me and the train roared off into the darkness, I sensed that this crew-cut cleric was destined to play a profound role in my life. I was soon to learn that earlier that evening, on the way to the banquet, he had asked, "Lord, you must have some reason for taking me to this dinner. What is it?" The moment he walked into the room and saw me, it was as if God said, "This man is the reason I have brought you here. He is open to the baptism in my Spirit."

The next week Bredesen appeared at our apartment in Queens. He had ridden a bicycle all the way from College Point through the heavy New York traffic to bring us a book on the baptism in the Holy Spirit. Needless to say, I was deeply impressed by this man's enthusiasm and commitment to Jesus Christ.

Harald began meeting with our prayer group at the seminary, and then in our homes. He also introduced us to a number of other prayer meetings that were being conducted in the area. My hunger for God grew even deeper.

Harald was teaching on the importance of water baptism. I had been baptized as a boy in the Baptist Church back home, but I knew it was not a believer's baptism. So I asked Harald to baptize me, which he did in First Baptist Church of Flushing. I came out of the water fully expecting Jesus to baptize me in the Holy Spirit just as he had been when he came out of the Jordan. But nothing happened.

The next week Harald invited our prayer group to the Flushing Full Gospel Church to meet with Arthur Graves, the pastor.

Our entire prayer group came and was astonished when halfway through the prayer meeting something happened to Harald. Suddenly he leaped to his feet, a torrent of beautiful words in a tongue I had never heard pouring from the depths of his being. To paraphrase Charles Finney, he "literally bellowed out the unutterable gushings of his heart." He seemed transported into another realm of experience. I didn't know what had happened to him. I only knew that God had touched his life.

On the way home to College Point he explained, "Pat, tonight for the first time I had an overwhelming desire to preach God's Word, to proclaim it from the housetops. As much as I have loved my present job, I know I can't be happy in it anymore. Tonight God has called me to preach."

Three days later Harald phoned to tell me God's next move in his life. He had been asked if he would accept a call to pastor the historic First Reformed Church in Mount Vernon, New York. He had never before heard about the First Reformed Church of Mount Vernon, New York. God had let us experience this dealing with his servant in order to heighten our expectancy of what he had in store for us.

We began holding all-night prayer meetings in the Bayside Methodist Church, and God dealt with us in new ways as he spoke to us individually, yet in the same way. Sometimes we would separate and go into various parts of the building to pray and read our Bibles. One night Dick Simmons, Dick White, and I had done this and then came back together to find God had given us all the same Scripture. We spent the rest of the night praising God for the breakthrough that must be at hand.

Soon after, Dick White called Harald Bredesen. "I have to leave tomorrow morning for an out-of-town trip," he said. "I desperately need to talk to you tonight."

"I can't make it tonight," Harald said, "but I have a friend of mine who might be able to help. His name is Paul Morris, and he is a Spirit-filled Presbyterian."

Dick went out to Paul Morris's church that night and stayed for a potluck supper. Afterward, Morris invited him to meet with the elders of the church. They read an article from a booklet called *Believing Is Receiving*, which dealt with how to be filled with the Holy Spirit. Then Paul said, "Well, Dick, would you like for me to pray for you?"

"Yes!"

Dick sat in a chair while the men laid hands on him. Then Paul began to pray. Dick said he had never heard a prayer like that before. It was like prophecy. As he prayed, Dick touched for the first time the limitless power of God. He was filled with the Holy Spirit. Haltingly at first, then with great fluency, he began to praise God in tongues. The assurance was his.

Dick had been a very somber person, but when he related his experience to me, I saw a new light in his face. I would never be satisfied until I had received the baptism for myself.

But things were growing tense at home again. Even though Dede seemed to be in harmony with the things of God, she was having her problems with those seeking the baptism. I sensed it, in particular, whenever the prayer group met at our apartment. Dick White and others who had received the baptism would begin praying and praising God, and the rest of us would join in. There would arise a chorus of "Praise the Lord! Hallelujah! Glory!" Invariably, when things got loud, Dede would excuse herself, saying she had to take care of one of the children. Only she never returned to the meetings.

"I enjoy the Bible study, Pat," she confessed, "but I have other things to do than sit in that room all night praising the Lord. You bring all these strange people into my home and then expect me to sit around and shout with them. I just can't do it."

"Honey," I pleaded, "be patient with me. God is pouring out his Spirit. He's moving in a supernatural way and I must follow him."

"It's not just that," Dede said. "You spend all your time running around the city, and your children never even know they have a father. Just because you never knew your father very well as a child is no excuse for you not spending time with your children."

A week later, still smarting under the guilt that Dede had poured out on me, I came home from school and found Tim running a high fever.

That evening, his temperature went up to 104° and by bedtime it was 105°. His skin was burning hot and dry. He was unconscious and having muscle spasms. Dede, who had tried unsuccessfully to get a doctor, exclaimed, "We've got to do something! He's on the verge of convulsions!"

I fell on my knees. "God, do something."

Dede put Elizabeth to bed and then got on her knees with me beside Tim. I laid my hands on him and cried out again. While I was pleading with God, it flashed into my mind what a lousy father I was.

How imperfect my love toward this little boy! As these thoughts flooded my mind, I was suddenly aware of how much God loved him. I was trying to get God to do something for my son, pleading with him to love him, while all the time he loved him far more than I ever could.

So, instead of begging anymore, I just consciously lifted Tim up to the Lord. I gave him back to God. Suddenly I was aware of the love of God enfolding him, and the power of God going through him. He opened his eyes and murmured, "Daddy, I gotta go to the bathroom."

He came back to his bed perspiring. I knew the fever had broken, and the healing was taking place.

"Thank you, Jesus," I began to weep. "Oh, thank you." I gradually realized I didn't have to ask him for anything. I could never, in a thousand lifetimes, talk him into anything that he didn't want to do. And there was no need to try anyway. He loved me—and Tim—with a perfect love. That was why he healed Tim. I felt waves of love flow over me as I began to give praise to Jesus. "Praise your Holy name!" I shouted. "Praise you, Jesus."

It was in this moment that I became aware my speech was garbled. I was speaking in another language. Something deep within me had been given a voice, and the Holy Spirit had supplied the words. I was aware of the sounds, but they were not of my own creation. It sounded like some kind of African dialect, and the flow of words continued on for five minutes or more.

Finally it subsided, and I was once again aware of Dede's presence in the room. She was sitting on the edge of the sofa bed, watching me. I lowered my hands and looked at her. She was wide-eyed.

"How long has this been going on?"

"What do you mean?" I answered.

"Praying in tongues."

"I just started. This was the first time."

I sat down beside her, and she reached over and gently took my hand. I felt a joining in the Spirit I hadn't felt in a long time. Softly she said, "You remember I said you didn't need to go running around all over the city seeking; I told you that God would give you the baptism right here in your own living room."

She was right.

He had.

VI

Insight into a Miracle

———
———
———

The date was March 22, 1959—my twenty-ninth birthday. The occasion was a party in my honor in the social hall of the Reformed Church in Mt. Vernon where I was now serving as an associate to Pastor Harald Bredesen.

It was almost 10:00 P.M. when the small group of seminary students left the social hall and gathered in the great Gothic sanctuary with its thick walls, massive arches, and stained-glass windows. There was just one light burning over the altar as we stood in a circle of fellowship, praying.

In those days we had a deep-seated fear of what church people would think of our experience with the Holy Spirit, and our prayer meetings were often held late at night, like a gathering of conspirators. As was true of the disciples after the crucifixion, we made a practice of locking the doors to our prayer meetings, "for fear of the Jews."

Suddenly, Harald began speaking in tongues. As he spoke, he began to clap his hands and to spin around in a tight circle. We realized that what was happening was supernatural and stood in quiet amazement as his pace quickened. He would speak a short phrase in tongues. Then he gave the interpretation in English. Then another phrase in tongues, with its interpretation. And then another. It seemed as if a heavenly teletype machine had mysteriously been activated. We pieced the message together:

"How long will you be bound by fear of men who themselves are the slaves of Satan? I am doing a new thing on the face of the earth. How long will you be silent? Declare the whole counsel of God. Hold nothing back. Hold nothing back!"

Everyone in the room knew we had heard from God. We waited in expectant silence.

Bredesen stopped still, paused for a moment, and then he said, "I think I should share the message of the charismatic move of the Holy Spirit with Mrs. Norman Vincent Peale."

I shook my head. Oh no, I thought, Harald is in the flesh now. He's being celebrity-conscious. "Harald, what in the world are you talking about?"

"Just this, Pat: God is telling me to go and share the message of his power and the baptism in the Holy Spirit with Mrs. Peale. I've had some church business with her. We are of the same denomination, you know."

"Well, we'll see, brother," I said, half-skeptically.

The next morning Dede and I were eating breakfast in our Queens apartment when the phone rang.

"What are you doing tonight?" It was Harald.

"What do you have in mind?"

"Are you free for dinner?"

"Well, yes, as far as I know."

"Well, we are having dinner with Mrs. Norman Vincent Peale."

"Uh huh," I said crinkling my forehead and smiling slightly. "And how is this going to happen?"

"This is God! She called me this morning about that church business. She said she was preparing to leave town and couldn't see me until her return. I told her I wanted to share something with her about what God is doing and she said, 'Well, if it is to be a sharing experience, I'll make time now. Could you come for dinner tonight?' "

That night Harald, Dick Simmons, and I had dinner with Mrs. Peale in her lovely Fifth Avenue apartment. During dinner we began relating what was happening. We told of the outpouring of the Holy Spirit all over the nation, and now hundreds of people were receiving the baptism in the Holy Spirit. We went ahead to relate how the Holy Spirit was manifesting himself through miracles, signs, wonders, and speaking in tongues. Mrs. Peale, her son, and younger daughter sat in rapt attention.

After dinner we went into the living room. There Mrs. Peale began to ask questions—interested questions. I felt an anointing of the Spirit, and began to share something of my personal experiences, and how I had received the manifestation of speaking in tongues. When I finished speaking, we began to pray, and under the unction of the Spirit Harald spoke in tongues. Dick Simmons gave the interpretation.

As the spirit of the moment subsided, I turned to look at Harald, but his chair was empty. He was gone. Harald had returned to the dining room where the Negro maid was cleaning the table. "You've got the Holy Ghost, haven't you?" he asked her. "Oh yes," she beamed. "We've been praying for this house for twenty years."

Mrs. Peale kept shaking her head saying, "This is difficult to believe, but I know it is of the Lord." She continued, "I wish I could stay, but I'm already late for an editorial meeting at *Guideposts*."

Ruth Peale was a little out of breath when she arrived at the regular Monday night editorial meeting at the *Guideposts* office. An interfaith magazine founded by Dr. Peale, *Guideposts* has offices located on the fifth floor of the same building that houses the Marble Collegiate Church.

Before she had her coat off, she asked the group assembled there, "Have you ever heard of 'speaking in tongues'?"

Some of those present said they had heard of it. A few thought it was an emotional outburst common to unlearned religious fanatics.

"Well, there were three men in my apartment tonight—the son of a U.S. Senator, a Reformed Church minister, and a Presbyterian minister—and they spoke in tongues. It was definitely not emotionalism. It was of God."

Present at the table was the senior editor of *Guideposts*, John Sherrill. John immediately began asking questions and asked to meet Harald. "He might be a good subject for a *Guideposts* story," he said.

The encounter produced far more than that; out of it came a book by John Sherrill entitled, *They Speak With Other Tongues*, the first best-seller on the charismatic renewal. It was to introduce hundreds of thousands to the baptism in the Holy Spirit.

While John was working on the book, Harald introduced him to Dave Wilkerson, founder of Teen Challenge. Dave had a great vision and great problems—he needed $10,000 for the work God had called him to do among street gangs. John introduced Dave to W. Clement Stone who has since given over $600,000 toward Dave's Teen Challenge ministry.

And out of this meeting came another book, the most widely read Christian book of the century—*The Cross and the Switchblade*, which has sold more than 10 million copies.

This and much more came out of our obedience to three words God had spoken—"Hold nothing back."

VII

Consulting the Oracles of God

———
———
———

It was Su Nae Chu, the Korean woman, who warned us against the foolishness of trying to force others to receive the baptism in the Holy Spirit. Sixteen students at Biblical Seminary had received the baptism, and we had grown confident, believing that we should go into all the churches around the country and convince others this was what they needed, too.

"No, no, no," Su Nae said, "you must never push people. That is the function of the Holy Spirit alone."

We decided we should let the Holy Spirit speak to others just as he had spoken to us—without our adding any undue pressure. This principle of temperance was to become a foundation stone in my ministry, one upon which I would continue to build for the rest of my life. We would preach Christ crucified, and while not denying the work of the Holy Spirit, we would not try to force the baptism upon anyone.

We did continue with our own search for the power of God, and I found God leading me into direct guidance. John Wesley referred to his quest for God's guidance when he wrote, "We consulted the oracles of God." For me a new dimension began to open.

Our initiation came in the form of Spirit-led worship. We would wait on God, and then he would give a psalm, a hymn, a prophecy, a portion of Scripture. On one occasion as we were praying, Dick White felt led to read a particular Psalm. While he was reading, the number of a hymn flashed in my mind. I was totally unfamiliar with the Presbyterian Hymnbook, but I picked it up and opened it to the page number that had come to my mind. There before my eyes was that particular Psalm set to music.

Such experiences in worship caused me to realize that God could lead me directly through the Scriptures and personal revelation. I recognized it as training for whatever ministry the Holy Spirit was preparing for me, even though I had no idea what that ministry was to be. All I knew was that it was to be the kind of ministry where I would often have to rely on just such revelations, and that this time was to be used in purifying myself so the percentage of error would grow less. To rely on this kind of direct guidance for your life's course, and not to have a clear channel, could lead to immediate disaster.

Now the seminary was beginning to put pressure on me. It was time for graduation, and I didn't have any work lined up. The seminary officials saw this as a reflection upon the school and were urging me to accept some church position. "When a young man graduates from seminary, he should immediately step into a church position," the dean told me. "But I can't understand you, Pat. Here you are with a wife and three small children, and you're doing nothing."

That wasn't quite accurate. I was working with Harald Bredesen as an associate pastor. I had been leading a Bible-study group for some Jewish Christians up in Westchester. I was considering the possibility of becoming a missionary to Israel, and I had contacted the Reformed Church of America (Harald's denomination) about a position as an evangelist.

It was the idea of missions that excited me most. I decided to explore every possible avenue. Having met a few missionaries associated with the Worldwide Evangelization Crusade and having been impressed with their dedication, I felt led to check out the possibilities there. One afternoon Dede and I left the children with friends and drove down to the WEC headquarters at Ft. Washington, Pennsylvania, just outside Philadelphia.

Driving along the banks of the Schuylkill River, we turned up the steep, winding road on the mountain behind the Christian Literature Crusade headquarters where Dr. Norman Grubb, head of the WEC, lived with his wife. Mrs. Grubb, daughter of famed missionary C.T. Studd, met us at the door of the apartment and ushered us into Dr. Grubb's study.

He was expecting us and offered us a seat at the far end of the room, apart from his cluttered desk and typewriter where he had produced so many books that had blessed the Christian world. Advanced in years and yet still active and healthy, he settled in an easy chair and listened to my presentation. Obviously, however, he had no leading from the Lord that I was to come as a missionary with WEC.

"Here we are," I said impatiently. "My wife is a graduate nurse. I have a law degree and will soon graduate from seminary, and we're both volunteering to go as missionaries. What would you like for us to do?"

"There's far more to missions than simply volunteering," he said in his English accent. "You have to be called."

"But we're desperate," I said. "We'll do anything God wants us to do."

"Even though you are both eminently qualified, it would be wrong for WEC to accept you as missionaries if God has other plans. We would, in essence, be standing in the way of God."

"But it seems a tragic waste for us to just sit around twiddling our thumbs," I argued futilely.

"It would be a far bigger tragedy for you to get into something God has not called you into," he said kindly. "For us to make a place for you with WEC just to make you happy would be a mistake. In fact, we have a place where you and your wife could serve right now. We need men and women like you, but only if God has called you specifically."

I got up and walked up and down the room, careful not to bump into the various artifacts that crowded his desks and shelves. "But the Bible says, 'Go ye into all the world and preach the Gospel to every creature,' and I have assumed that is my call to missions."

"No, no," Dr. Grubb said, clasping his hands in front of him, his white moustache bristling. "God's written Word is the *general* guide to his people; but remember, Pat, the Spirit gives the guidance, not the Book."

Dr. Grubb got up from his chair and put his arm around my shoulders, signaling it was time for us to go. "God calls all his people to go into the world and preach the Gospel to every creature. Now it's up to you to wait on the specific direction. I sense his call to you will be in ways quite different from any others in the past."

We walked to the door and stood on the concrete stoop. The huge trees towered above the house, and the wall of greenery shut out most of the sound of the busy traffic on the turnpike in the valley below. "I believe God has great things in store for you in the near future. Wait on him and pray. One day you will thank him that WEC did not stand in his way by taking you on as missionaries."

And so another door was shut. Yet it seemed that a far better door was swinging open in New York.

I was being considered as a candidate for a large church located around the corner from The Barbizon, a women's hotel on New York's upper east side. This particular church had the added appeal of a large parsonage, which to me at that time represented the height of luxury. I tried to kid myself that God wanted me to take the church, but in the inner recesses of my heart the question formed, "Do you really think that a luxurious parsonage is a call from me?" When the pulpit committee issued the call for me to come as their pastor, I said, "I'm sorry, but the Lord just hasn't given me any leading to accept. I'll have to refuse."

The chairman was taken aback. "We'll raise your salary," he offered.

"That's just the problem," I tried to explain.

They left, shaking their heads.

I had learned another lesson.

A month before graduation I was invited to preach at the Classan Avenue Presbyterian Church in Brooklyn. The church was one of the old nineteenth-century preaching centers that held fourteen hundred people. It had a horseshoe-shaped auditorium with a pulpit that projected out over the people like a balcony. The pulpit committee liked me and asked me to come as their pastor.

The church was located at the corner of Monroe and Classan Avenue in Bedford Stuyvesant, second only to Harlem as the worst black slum in America and located only a few blocks from where David Wilkerson was later to open his Teen Challenge Center. The parsonage was an old brownstone located several doors down from the church. The members, most of whom had moved out of the area, were in conflict with the members of the community who lived all around the church building but didn't attend. Walking through the ghetto community, I kept remembering the words of Stacey Woods that had challenged my heart when he spoke at Campus in the Woods: "If Jesus were born today, he probably would be born in one of the slums of New York."

Could it be, Lord, that you are calling me to a slum ministry? Is this the reason you told me to turn down the affluent church with the fancy parsonage?

But there was no peace when I told God that I was willing to accept the Classan Avenue Church. Therefore, I recommended Dick Simmons, who by now was taking graduate study at New York University while he worked as superintendent of a children's home in Fort Lee, New Jersey.

Dick's face blanched when I told him. "What's the trouble?" I asked.

"Last week," he said in a slow, thoughtful voice, "I was praying, and the Lord said, 'I'm going to send you to a place for which you have no natural desire.' While I was pastoring in Tucson I remember telling the Lord, 'Lord, the one place I don't want to go is the slums of Brooklyn.' Now you're telling me I might be called right to the place I don't want to go."

But after preaching there a couple of Sundays, Dick knew God was calling him right there. He resigned his position at the children's home and accepted the pastorate of the church, moving into the huge old brownstone manse that hadn't been occupied in years.

A week after the Simmonses moved in, Dede made her first—and what she intended to be her last—trip into Brooklyn. She dressed little Gordon, who was less than a year old, in his red knit suit and took him with her. He was clean and pretty when they left our apartment, but three hours later when Dede returned, she was in tears—and Gordon looked like he had been dumped in an ash heap.

"What happened?"

"Nothing," Dede said. "I just put him down on that filthy floor while Barb and I talked, and now look at him. That is the filthiest, ugliest, most germ-infested place I've ever been in. How in the world the city, much less the church, would allow anyone to live in a place like that is beyond me. I'll never go back. Never. I feel grimy just from the air over there.

"I'll tell you one thing," she shouted as she hurried to the shower, "if I were Barbara Simmons, I'd walk out for good!"

Three weeks after I graduated, Dede was called home to Columbus, Ohio, to nurse her brother, Ralph, who was recovering from a kidney operation. I decided to use the time to stay in New York and wait on the Lord in our apartment.

July in New York was hot and steamy, and for three weeks I sat in our apartment, fasting a part of the time, and seeking the plan of God for my life. One evening, the first week of July, I was sitting in our darkened living room praying when I heard a voice in my mind say, "Luke 12:33."

I put it aside and continued praying, asking God for guidance. Again I had the strong impression, "Luke 12:33."

I racked my brain trying to remember what that particular Scripture was, but could not remember. Switching on the lamp beside my chair, I reached for my Bible. The apartment was quiet, with only the faint sound of traffic on the street below. Relaxing in the easy chair, I flipped through the pages until I found the verse: "Sell all that ye have, and give alms . . ."

"Lord," I prayed, sitting upright and speaking aloud, "is this what you're trying to tell me to do?" But even as I asked, I knew the answer. It was.

I glanced around the apartment, at the wall-to-wall carpet, the beautiful Early American furniture, the pictures on the walls, and the silver on the buffet. "Lord, you know I'm not in bondage to material things. I even turned down that church job because it paid too much and had a comfortable parsonage. These things aren't standing in the way of my hearing your voice."

"I want you ready to move," the answer came back.

I glanced again at the Bible in my lap. The words leaped off the page and burned themselves on my consciousness. "Sell all you have and give alms . . ."

The next morning I wrote Dede a brief note. "God has been speaking to me through Luke 12:33."

In less than a week I had Dede's answer. I looked in amazement at her letter. "Honey, you do whatever the Lord tells you to do," she wrote.

That afternoon I put an ad in the paper:

For sale: Early American furniture, hand-rubbed.

The apartment was mobbed by potential buyers, and in less than two days I had sold everything we owned except the baby bed, a few pots and pans, Dede's clothes, a few silver pieces we had been given for wedding presents, and our seven-year-old DeSoto. I called the landlord, told him I was moving out, packed the rest of our belongings, and moved into the brownstone parsonage in Brooklyn with Dick and Barbara Simmons.

I gave some of the money I received from selling the furniture to Bob Pierce, director of World Vision, to help with his orphanages in Korea. I had $400 left. I felt I should give the rest to Dick Simmons to distribute among the poor.

"Dick," I said, "I've been led to give you some money."

"How much?" he asked as we stood in front of the old house.

"Four hundred dollars," I said. "Do with it as the Lord leads you."

We were standing on the sidewalk, and Dick looked up with the strangest expression on his face. "See all those things piled up on the street down there?" he asked, pointing across the street. I glanced in the direction he pointed and saw where a family had been dispossessed of their home. All their clothes were piled in apple crates on the sidewalk.

"I have been asking the Lord for some money to give to them," Dick said.

I grinned, shook my head, and emptied my wallet. "Praise the Lord," I said. "For the first time in my life I've given away everything. I'm completely broke."

I did have a few belongings left, things I hadn't sold. Dick helped me make a frame platform, and we piled them in the basement (we called it the catacombs) of the old house. It was a good thing we made the platform, for that night we had a flash flood, and the catacombs half filled with water. Only the platform saved the rest of my belongings.

On Friday of the next week Dede tried to call me from Columbus. The operator informed her the phone in our apartment had been disconnected and my calls were being taken at the residence of Dick Simmons in Brooklyn.

Dede was panicky and telephoned Dick's home.

"Barbara, where's Pat?" Dede asked when the phone was answered.

"He's here," she said.

"What's he doing there?" she asked, her voice beginning to show some strains of tension.

"You mean you don't know?"

"No, I don't know! I never know anything he does. Let me speak to him."

When I took the phone, Dede was almost hysterical. "Pat, what's going on there? What's happened?"

"I sold the furniture," I answered.

"You what?" she screamed. "Oh, Pat, what have you done this time?"

"Didn't you read my letter?" I asked, puzzled.

"What letter?"

"The letter where I told you God was speaking to me through Luke 12:33."

"Pat, I don't even know what Luke 12:33 is! Why have you sold the furniture? Why are you living with Dick and Barbara?"

"But you wrote back and told me I should do whatever the Lord was telling me to do. And he told me through Luke 12:33 to sell the furniture and give all the money to the poor."

"You mean, you gave the money away, too?"

"Well, yes, that's what the Scripture said."

"Oh Pat, I didn't read that verse. I never look up verses that people scribble down like that."

"Honey, I'm sorry, but you should have looked up that one, because it's too late now."

"You mean everything's gone?"

"Yep, and I've given all the money away and moved in here with Dick and Barbara."

There was a long silence on the other end of the line, and I heard her crying, softly at first and then almost out of control. "Pat," she sobbed, "I just can't take any more. I left you there to look after things while I was gone and you . . ." Her voice trailed off in convulsive sobs. "What can we do now?" she finally choked out.

"I feel the Lord is calling me to go home to my friends and tell them what great things God has done for me," I said. "That's Mark 5:19."

"Great things?" Dede exclaimed, her anger swelling up through her tears like flames bursting through rolling smoke.

I picked Dede up on Wednesday, and we drove in icy silence across the sweltering countryside from Columbus to Lexington, Virginia. The fact that she left some of her personal things in Columbus rather than taking them with her indicated that one more straw would break the camel's back, and she would leave—for good.

I was bothered, but filled with a deep assurance that I was doing what God wanted, regardless of how ridiculous it seemed.

We arrived in Lexington Friday night, and Saturday morning one of mother's friends who belonged to a small Bible Presbyterian Church called. The pastor was on vacation, and they wanted me to preach. I consented.

The Sunday evening service at the church was followed by a radio broadcast. Some of the men were excited about the message. "We think this is so good, we'd like to sponsor you all week long on a radio broadcast," one of them said.

I was delighted. I had never spoken on radio before, and it gave me an opportunity to share the Gospel for fifteen minutes every afternoon in my hometown, fulfilling the command I felt I had received in Brooklyn to go home to my friends and tell them what great things God had done for me.

Monday of that week I came home, and Mother handed me a letter. "This came this afternoon," she said. "I thought you might be interested in it."

"Who's it from?"

"Do you remember George Lauderdale? He was in school with you sixteen years ago. Now he's a pastor with the Associate Reformed Presbyterian Church in Norfolk. I've corresponded with him occasionally, and he's added a P.S. to this letter that involves you."

I took the letter and looked at the bottom of the page. "There is a television station in Portsmouth, Virginia, that has gone defunct and is on the market. Would Pat be interested in claiming it for the Lord?"

VIII

The Spirit Gives Guidance

It was one of God's coincidences.

Two days after seeing George Lauderdale's unusual letter, I left the house to drive to the radio station for my fifteen-minute broadcast. On the way I stopped for a light. Glancing up, I saw a smiling, black-haired fellow standing at the curb. It was as if a figure out of my past had suddenly materialized before me.

"George Lauderdale!" I called, jumping out of the car. "What are you doing here?"

"The Lord brought me," he said, throwing his arm around my shoulders.

I was dumbfounded. "Last night I had a vision," he said. "I don't have things like this very often, but it was a man from Lexington, saying 'Come up here. You haven't finished your work here.' So I got in my car early this morning and drove the 240 miles up from Norfolk. I've just pulled in."

I took him with me up to the radio station where he assisted me with the program. Afterward we talked over a cup of coffee in a corner drugstore. "I saw your letter two days ago," I said. "Tell me about this station in Portsmouth."

"All I know is that it is a UHF station that has gone off the air and is on the block. I began wondering how it could be used for the Lord, and you came to my mind."

"But that's ridiculous," I said. "I know absolutely nothing about

[65]

television. I've never even owned a television set. How much does it cost to erect a station like that?"

"Oh, between $250,000 and $300,000."

"Where could I get that kind of money?" I blurted out.

"It will sell for much less than that," George said. "Besides, the Lord can supply the need."

"But what about programs?"

"Oh, the Lord will supply the programs, too."

I listened but wasn't convinced.

That evening, still mulling over George Lauderdale's proposal, I walked out into a field near our house. It was the same field where I had played football as a young boy. The smell of honeysuckle filled the air, and the sky was bright with a million stars. Walking over the soft grass, I looked up and began to pray.

"Lord, I don't know a thing about television. I've never had a drama course in my life. I hardly know a camera from a receiver . . ."

I paused, listening to the silence around me.

"Lord," I heard myself praying, "if you want me to take over that station, tell me how much it will cost."

Immediately a figure came to mind. It was $37,000. That was a far cry from the $300,000 that the station was supposedly worth, but God might as well have said $37 million as far as my resources were concerned. Yet so sure was I that the figure came from God that I began praising him for it. It was not my figure. I had not sat down and arrived at it logically. It was God's figure, given to me when I allowed his Holy Spirit to pray through me. I said, "Thank you, Lord," and returned to the house.

That night, after the children were in bed, I told Dede what had transpired. I told her about George Lauderdale and about the figure of $37,000. "I'm going to write the owner tomorrow," I concluded.

Dede sighed and shook her head. No longer angry, just tired and resigned, she said, "Pat, we don't even own a television set, remember? Now you're talking about buying an entire station. And with what? We don't have a dime. We're living like Gypsies. If it weren't for the generosity of your parents, we'd be in the poorhouse. You're a dreamer if you think you can raise $37,000 to buy a TV station."

I quoted George Lauderdale: "The Lord will provide."

She pursed her lips and stared helplessly at the ceiling. "Before now, Pat, when you got the wrong hymn from a hymnbook because someone had given a wrong prophecy, no great harm was done. But when you begin getting figures about how much to pay for a television station, then you can get in big trouble—not that we're not already in trouble."

I knew Dede was right. But I also knew God had spoken to me. I had learned to know his voice. And I knew beyond doubt this was God's figure.

The next morning I wrote Mr. Tim Bright, the owner of the station. "I understand you have a television station for sale. Will you please tell me how much you want for it."

The day before we left to return to New York, Bright's answer was in the mail. "For the equipment, building, and land I want $50,000. For the equipment alone I want $25,000."

My heart leaped. God's figure was right in the middle.

My thoughts went back to the Marine Corps. To obtain the necessary coordinates, Marine Corps artillery gunners were taught bracketing. They would fire one round beyond the target, then fire one round short. Then, on the third, they fired a barrage right smack in the middle. It was called firing for effect. Tim Bright had bracketed the deal. God had fired for effect.

I showed the letter to Dede. "Look!" I shouted. "God hit it right in the middle."

"Yes," she replied. "But we haven't got any part of $37,000, and you know it."

She was right. We had no choice but to return to the splendors of Classan Avenue.

IX

Rats, Roaches, and Bedbugs

———
———
———

"Pat, I just can't," Dede said. "All the way up here I kept telling myself this was just temporary, but I just can't stand it." She hugged little Gordon, our third child, to her and drew back into the car.

Our 1953 DeSoto was parked in front of the brownstone parsonage on Classan Avenue, our prospective home for the next two months. It was a hot September day. Perspiration was running down my forehead as I looked out. A row of elm trees bore silent witness to the grandeur of a former age. Now the street and sidewalks were littered with battered furniture, broken bottles, and assorted trash. Blacks were sitting on the steps in front of their brownstone tenements, drinking beer. The architectural facade of this once-fashionable Brooklyn street was much like it had been a hundred years ago, but inside each stately brownstone, blacks and Puerto Ricans were living five or ten to a room in indescribable squalor.

Slum landlords have a high turnover of tenants and Bedford Stuyvesant, our new neighborhood, must have led the field. Day after day, indigent black families were thrown bag and baggage into the dirty streets. Beds, mattresses, chairs, and tables would be heaped in a pathetic pile along the sidewalk, to be scavenged by passing gangs of vandals and strewn over the street.

I felt a dull, sinking sensation in the pit of my stomach. In the words of Job, "The fear I feared had come upon me."

"We can't stay out here," I said to her. "Let's get on inside. Dick said they had a room for us on the third floor."

"A room?" Dede said in unbelief. "Pat, we've got three children—and we're supposed to stay in *a* room!"

"Actually it's more like a room and a half."

"Well, it can't be any worse inside than it is out here," she said stoically as she climbed out of the car.

We were not the only visitors living in the house. In fact, it had become something of a hotel for the friendless, with Dick Simmons as manager and Barbara as housemother. Besides us, there were Dick White and Alice Blair from the seminary. They had graduated along with us and were now living by faith also. Then across the hall from our room and a half was a tiny room that housed a huge black man from Jamaica whom Dick had invited to come live with us. He was an amiable psychotic, a tall hulk of a man with gangling limbs and a cavernous mouth filled with shining white teeth. Barbara warned us that he sometimes rambled through the house at night, singing at the top of his voice, but that basically he was harmless, although sometimes Dick had to handle him by cuffing his ears.

That night at dinner, which was served in the catacombs, we met the rest of the boarders who either lived in the house or took meals with us. The first was a badly crippled young man with a spastic condition that caused him to stagger and shake. He had been an object of the charity of Jerome Hines, the Metropolitan Opera star, and somehow Dick had heard of him and invited him to the house. Moreover, the young man had been dating a spastic girl—and had gotten her pregnant. Now the girl, great with child, was an occasional boarder. Both of them had a terrible time getting around and unintentionally threw food all over the table when they ate.

Oddly enough, Dede wasn't affected by any of this. As a nurse she had a natural compassion for those who were crippled. But there were other things that disturbed her . . .

The ambling black man would sometimes laugh uproariously when the spastics threw food on the table. That first night Dick Simmons reached across the table and slapped the black giant in the face, trying to get him to stop laughing. The good-natured fellow just shouted louder, "Praise the Lord!"

Then there was Ruby, the madam from the brothel next door. For a month Dick and Barbara had been praying that the Lord would close the house, since men were coming in and out at all times of the day and night. Three days before we arrived, the madam of the house had a vision. Christ appeared to her and told her to get out of the prostitution business. But when she tried, she was physically attacked by demons and went running down the street, tearing her clothes and screaming, "Get them away from me! They're biting me all over!"

The neighbors were terrified. They caught her, opened the front door of the manse, and shoved her in. Simmons came down the stairs and found her crouched against the wall, rolling her eyes and clenching her teeth.

"What's wrong?" he asked.

"Oh, they've got me eggs. Coffee with eggs in them. They's biting me inside."

Dick tried to approach her but she crouched tighter in the corner and screamed. "Get away. They's choking me. I've got snakes coming out my throat."

Dick White joined Simmons and they started across the room toward her, hands outstretched, shouting at the demons and commanding them to come out in the name of Jesus. Ruby threw her hands in the air as if hit by a high-voltage line. Her hair stood straight out on her head, and her face lit up with a bright radiance. "JESUS!" she screamed. "JESUS!" Then a deep peace settled over her, and she leaned against the sofa, completely delivered.

Now beautiful and "clothed in her right mind" Ruby, too, was taking her meals at the parsonage. She had closed down her operation and soon after lost her house because she no longer had enough money to make the usurious contract payments on it.

In addition to these, there were other people who wandered in for meals. Most of these were "Carolina Negroes," blacks who had been kicked out of their houses or apartments and had no place to go, nothing to eat. Dick's compassion knew no bounds. It constantly challenged and convicted me.

The first night we were there, Dick Simmons and I were called out on the street to assist a black family who had been evicted from their apartment for nonpayment of rent. All their belongings were being thrown out on the sidewalk. We went up to help them get their stuff out of the apartment; it was the filthiest place I had ever seen. The stench was so strong I almost gagged. The grease in the kitchen was so thick you could scrape it off with a knife, and the building was filled with flies, thousands of them. We stored the family's meager belongings beside mine in the catacombs, and they joined us for meals at the house.

That night I prayed, "Lord, I belong to you. I'll do anything you say. Please don't take too long to teach me your will."

We started the next day with a prayer and worship session between five and six o'clock. Since Dick was in charge of the house, the rest of us felt we had to be in submission to him. From six to seven we had a Spirit-led worship service where we would wait for God to speak to us. From seven to seven-thirty we had a time of intercessory prayer where we mostly prayed aloud in the Spirit. We finally had breakfast at eight.

Meals were rather out of the ordinary. During the day we went down to the market on 1st Avenue after the general marketing day was over, getting free vegetables by the case. Mostly we were eating what we called "tribulation food," made up of soybeans, which we bought in two-bushel sacks. One of us had read somewhere that by analysis, if not by taste, soybeans are the perfect food. If that was so, we had a perfect diet. We had every kind of soybean concoction imaginable: soybean soup, soybean soufflé, soybean mush, soybean patties. We also mixed the soybeans with a case of rutabagas and ate the rutabagas with various kinds of vegetables. Meat was difficult to obtain, so we lived mostly as vegetarians—not by conviction but by necessity.

The second night, as we sat in the catacombs eating our tribulation food, there was a loud snap from behind the washing machine. Dede jumped out of her chair. "What was that?"

Simmons reached around behind the washer and pulled out a huge rattrap holding a dead rat. It seems we had arrived back in New York at just the time the rats came out into the city in full force. At first, Dick had decided to poison the rats, but all he succeeded in doing was driving them into the walls where they died. The stench had been so bad they could hardly stand it, so they decided it was better to live with live rats than dead ones.

That same night, Dede woke up in the middle of the night screaming. I tried to calm her, but she leaped out of bed and began jumping up and down in the middle of the floor and shaking her head. She was brushing herself frantically and screaming, "They're all over me! They're crawling all over me!"

"You've been dreaming," I said. "I don't see anything on you."

I pulled her to me and held her tight, feeling her body trembling under her nightgown. "It's all right," I whispered. "Don't wake up the baby. It's just a bad dream."

I felt her body relax as she snuggled against me, her warm face pressed against my chest. "Come on back to bed. It's just Satan's trick to scare you."

But Dede was not the only one to have problems that night. Dick Simmons reported that he was coming under attack by demons.

"How can you be sure, Dick?" I asked.

He held out his arms. "Do you see these red welts? Late at night the attack gets so bad that I literally claw at my flesh. I have jumped out of my bed to look for the attacker, but nothing is ever there. I'm not sure I can stand this thing much longer."

I looked closely at his inflamed arms, "Dick, that's not from demons," I said smugly. "I've been reading a book about nutrition; those welts are caused by a serious vitamin A deficiency."

"Vitamin deficiency nothing," he said defensively. "By now I think I should be capable of recognizing an attack of Satan."

"Okay, have it your way," I said as I turned to leave; "but this time a vitamin pill is your answer."

As Dick's welts spread to other parts of his body, he besought the Lord with great fervor to bring deliverance from the attack of the enemy. I, in my turn, besought Dick to change his diet.

Late one night Dick bellowed up the stairs, "Pat, come down— quick!" I raced downstairs and met a shamefaced leader. "Here are my demons and your vitamin deficiency," he laughed, as he pointed to the back of his bed. "We bought this furniture from the Salvation Army—and it's alive with bedbugs. I guess they always got away before I could catch them!"

Later we discovered that the entire house was "under attack." The day before, the sanitation department had fumigated the former brothel next-door to us. Instead of killing the bugs, however, they had simply chased all the roaches and vermin over into our house. We spent the rest of the day going around the house with spray cans, spraying every nook and cranny. "I guess sometimes God wants us to spray as well as pray," Dick White cracked.

Even though the old house was still vermin and rat infested, it had been cleaned up considerably since Dick and Barbara first moved in. A thick coat of paint can cover a multitude of evils, and the church, not wanting their pastor to live in filth, had at least added a lot of paint.

It was the situation in the community that distressed us, for despite our efforts to evangelize, we didn't seem to be making much headway. Daylight hours were spent going out on the streets talking to the neighbors about Jesus Christ, or setting up our microphones, amplifiers, and loudspeakers, and holding street services. At night you could hear the vandals running up and down the sidewalks, stripping cars, slamming bedsteads into the street, and throwing around the furniture belonging to the families that had been evicted.

At the end of the block, a man had come home drunk and began a search through the apartment for his wife who was fearfully hiding from him. He found her in a closet, and threw her out of a fourth-story window. Her body smashed to its death onto the concrete sidewalk near the place where we did our preaching.

Right behind the parsonage there had been two knifings, one by a man and the other by a woman. Yet we lived in no particular fear for our own safety. Our greatest concern arose when Barbara Simmons' mother came up from Alabama to visit us. Like my own mother, Barb's mother was horrified that we were living in the midst of one of the largest black ghettos in America. Thanks to her Alabama training, she had but one word for dark-skinned people. She used the word "nigger" over and over, despite our objections. Even though our relations with the black citizenry had been peaceful, we were all suddenly on edge, fearing the intrusion of a segregationist in our midst would cause strife and conflict.

All went well until our five-year-old Tim picked up some of the Alabama jargon and carried it with him out on the street. "Hey, you little nigger boy," we heard him shout one afternoon as he was playing on the sidewalk in front of the brownstone.

Horrified, I grabbed Tim and pulled him inside. We stood behind the closed door, peering through the window, waiting to see if a race riot was going to begin, but nothing happened. Fortunately we found it far easier to explain to Tim about his vocabulary than it was to explain to Barbara's mother about hers. When soon thereafter she returned to Alabama, we all breathed a bit easier.

All of these things I could take; but Dede's rebellion bothered me. Thrust into a group of "fanatics" and unable to become a part of our fellowship for fear of becoming like us, she withdrew more and more into a shell. The explosion came on the first of October when Dick

Simmons, as presiding elder, announced at breakfast, "Today is bath day. Everyone has to take a bath today."

"I have a will of my own," Dede shot back at him across the table. "No one is going to tell me when to bathe or not to bathe."

Dick's stubborn streak flared. "As elder of this house, I set the rules and expect everyone here to follow them. Not only is this bath day, but I'm also calling a fast for the rest of the day."

"Now wait a minute." Dede's temper flamed up. "If God wants me to fast, he'll have to tell me himself."

Dick was not used to this kind of rebellion on the part of his subjects. Looking very stern, he turned to Dede and declared, "When I announce a fast, everyone fasts."

Dede looked across the table at me. "Pat, I need three dollars."

"What for?" I asked innocently.

"If the rest of the fools in this house are going without food just because one fanatic demands it, that's all right for them. But I'm going out to buy some hamburger so my children can get their daily nutritional requirements."

"Now just a minute, Dede," Dick said, rising from the table. "I called this fast, and I intend to enforce it."

"Then start enforcing it," Dede shot back. "I take orders only from my husband and from the Lord. If you want Pat to tell me to do something, then you talk to Pat. But I'm not one of your slaves."

Furious, Dick looked at me, but all I could do was shrug my shoulders. It seemed wiser not to get further involved.

"I want you to come to my office, Dede, and we'll talk about this," Dick said.

"There's nothing to talk about. God told you to fast, but he didn't tell me. It's as simple as that."

There was a long period of silence at the table, and finally Dick began to back down. Very few people, myself included, were a match for Dede when her Irish temper flared. "All right. We'll have a no-pleasant-bread fast then."

"A what?" she said.

"A no-pleasant-bread fast."

"What's that?"

"No dessert," Dick said.

Dede began to laugh. "That's great. Just great. We haven't had any dessert in three weeks. All we've had has been greens, sweet potatoes, and soybeans."

Dick blushed, and Dede got up from the table—her point secure. That morning she went out and bought hamburger, which we mixed with soybeans for lunch.

The only progress I could see on Dede's part was her involvement in our predawn prayer meetings, which had finally begun to take on a spiritual tone. In fact, Harald Bredesen and others from outside the city often joined us, and we would sit around the living room for an hour worshiping the Lord and letting Him speak to us. During these times, Dede seemed to soften. One in the group would have a Scripture, and then another would call out a Scripture passage. As we turned to it, we found it would be on exactly the same subject as the first one mentioned. Sometimes someone would announce a hymn number, and we would find it to be the same Scripture set to music. There would be tongues and interpretation followed by prophecy and sometimes exhortation from the group. Even though the meetings sometimes got loud as we praised the Lord, more and more I found Dede joining in.

The spiritual climax began the second week of October. For several weeks we had been discussing having a water baptism service. Dede remained cool toward the entire matter, saying that she had been baptized as a Roman Catholic and there was no need for repetition. Yet as we discussed it at our daily meetings, I found Dede showing more interest.

"Pat," she said one night after we had gone to our room, "you know I'm just not with this spiritual business very much. It's not that I don't want to be. I really want to hear from God. Maybe I should be obedient to Jesus concerning water baptism."

I wanted to shout. It was a major breakthrough, not only in Dede's outward willingness to involve herself in the Holy Spirit, but in her willingness to submit herself to my spiritual headship. I reached over and pulled her to me, thanking God for this surrender.

The change in Dede's attitude came just at the right time, for her mother arrived the next day from Europe. She called from a downtown hotel, and we invited her out for dinner at the house. I prayed triply hard that the Holy Spirit would give the necessary grace.

She arrived that evening and expressed the same horror at our living quarters that Dede had expressed when she first moved onto Classan Avenue. She was astonished that her daughter, with a master's degree in nursing, had allowed her sorry husband to move her into this roach-infested slum.

The girls put together a special meal for her, and then we sat and talked.

"Dede, I'm leaving in the morning for Columbus, and I want you and the children to come with me. There's no sense in you staying on in this squalor."

I felt my stomach tighten as I awaited Dede's answer. She spoke gently but firmly. "Mother, for the first time in my life I realize if I leave Pat, I would not only be leaving my husband, but leaving the Lord. God is more important to me than anything else in the world, and I cannot turn my back on him."

"You mean to sit there and tell me that God is more important to you than the welfare of your children?"

"God will take care of my children," Dede said kindly. "But even if he doesn't, I must still follow him."

That night, after Dede's mother had returned to the hotel, we knelt together in prayer. I remembered something I had learned: commitment always precedes revelation. Dede had made her commitment. God's glorious revelation was sure to follow.

Saturday afternoon, October 13, was the most beautiful day of the year. The air was balmy with just a touch of autumn. The leaves were at the height of their glory, giving a backdrop of fantastic color as we drove out to Long Island Sound for the baptismal service. Harald was along and had provided the black baptismal robes. We formed a car caravan from the manse, since there were several others to be baptized, including the former madam and the spastic boy who had since married his pregnant girl friend.

We found a deserted place on the shore of the sound, and had a cookout before gathering at the waterside. Paul Morris and his wife, Helen, had come to be baptized since he had never been immersed in water. Dede willingly consented that Harald should be the one to immerse her.

We stood in a semicircle at the edge of the calm water which was rippled only now and then by the autumn breeze. Far out in the sound a tugboat sounded its lonely horn, which was the only thing to keep me from believing we were standing on the shore of the Sea of Galilee two thousand years before. One by one the candidates entered the water. Harald baptized Paul, and then the two of them took Dede out about waist deep into the sound and gently lowered her beneath the water. As she came up, her hair dripping wet around her face, I thought she was the most beautiful creature I had ever seen. The glow of the Lord was all around her, and my eyes filled with tears as I waded out to walk back to shore with her.

Dede and the others went back to the beach to change their clothes, and Paul reappeared first. We were standing facing the water, with the sun to our backs. A communion service had been prepared, but before it was served, the Spirit of the Lord fell on Paul and he began to prophesy. Even though his face was turned to heaven, I knew the words were for me.

"You shall go forth and minister to thousands, yes, to tens of thousands, and the blessing of the Lord shall be upon you."

I was overcome with joy and felt the glory of the Lord descending upon me. Then Paul turned to me and said, "The Lord has just given me faith for your television ministry. It shall come to pass. I know it and I believe it, and I now claim it before God."

Once again the tears poured from my eyes as I dropped to my knees in the sand. Afterward we stood at the water's edge, breaking a common loaf and drinking from a common cup as Harald repeated the familiar words of Jesus, "For this is my blood of the new covenant which is shed for many for the remission of sins."

It was a holy moment as each of us stood alone in the presence of God. Unknown to me at the time, Dede, who was but a few feet from me, was having her own experience with the Lord.

X

Midnight Revelations

———
———
———

I don't know how long I slept, but I was awakened about midnight. Dede had attended a Bible study at Paul Morris' church and had not come in when I went to bed. Now the streetlight was shining through the window that faced Classan Avenue, shedding a soft light over the entire room. I looked up and saw Dede kneeling at the foot of our bed, speaking in the most beautiful language I had ever heard. It sounded like French—but I knew it was tongues—and I knew she was praising the Lord. The light was to her back, yet her face was aglow with a light that surrounded her body. I was almost afraid to breathe for fear of breaking the spell of that beautiful moment.

I slipped out from under the covers and knelt on the floor beside her. I sensed she knew I was there, but her prayer language never faltered or ceased. Softly I joined her, praying in tongues as the Spirit gave utterance.

It seems that we were there only moments, joined in the Spirit in a profoundly mystical way, but I know it was for a long time. Normally Dede complained of kneeling on the hard floor, and sometimes my knees got sore, too. But this night, with the baby asleep in the crib behind us and the light from the streets of New York filtering through the windows, there was no weariness, only glory.

Finally the tongues ceased, and we knelt in silence, drinking in the indescribable beauty of that holy moment. Then I said softly, "When? When did it happen?"

"Tonight at the Bible study," Dede said, leaning forward on her knees and resting her elbows on the bed. "I was listening to the teacher instruct us on how to pray in tongues. He said, 'If you know you have been filled with the Holy Spirit, then automatically you should be able to speak in tongues. In fact, any of the manifestations of the Spirit are potentially yours.' After the meeting, he laid hands on all of us and told us to go home and kneel down and tell the Lord how much we loved him. He said we should speak out in faith the first word that came to our mind, regardless of how strange it sounded. I came in here, knelt down, spoke the first sound in faith, and suddenly a whole language began to flow from within."

"You mean you received the baptism in the Holy Spirit tonight?" I asked.

"Oh no," Dede said, laying her head over on the foot of the bed. "I received that the other day out on the beach at the water baptismal service."

"But why didn't you tell me?"

"I was afraid to," she said shyly. "You know everyone around here says you have to speak in tongues the minute you receive the baptism, or it isn't real. I was afraid they would make fun of my experience, and it was so precious that I just kept it inside."

"What happened out there?"

"It was after the communion service," Dede said, reaching over and entwining her fingers in mine as the angelic glow continued to shine from her. "I had asked Barbara and Alice to look after the children, and I had come back down the beach to stand where everyone was singing and praising the Lord. As I praised him, suddenly it was as if no one else were there. Everything turned to gold around me—the sky, the water, and the sand all blended together as though they were made of perfect gold. I felt myself ascending up into the presence of the Lord, and his glory surrounded me. There was glory everywhere."

"Oh Pat," she said, lifting her head from the bed, "it was indescribable. It seemed as if I was caught up into the very glory of God."

"How long did it last?"

"Not long. There was glory everywhere, and then out of the corner of my eye I saw Gordon running toward the water. I said, 'Lord, I'll be right back,' and I ran and caught him. While I was gone, Paul asked all those who wanted to receive the baptism to kneel. By the time I got back, they were already back on their feet. I was too late."

"But you really weren't too late."

"That's right; Jesus had already baptized me in his Holy Spirit."

The next morning I shared with Dede a concern that had been growing on my heart. "It just may be that God wants us to stay here in Brooklyn. Would you be willing?"

"I thought we settled that the other day," Dede grinned.

"I have to make some kind of decision about the house next-door. I've been thinking about borrowing the money to buy it and convert it into a mission to help these people."

"You mean the old brothel?" Dede grinned.

I blushed and nodded my head.

"If that is what God wants us to do, I'll be willing; but what about the television station? Have you prayed about that?"

I had prayed. Often. Daily. But I had to settle this thing about the house first.

That night I went downstairs, out the front door, and around to the side door of the church building. There was a single sixty-watt bulb burning over the altar, and I went inside, sat cross-legged on the floor in the semidark auditorium, and prayed, "Lord, do you want us to buy that house and stay here?"

Immediately I had an impression in my mind. "Jeremiah 16:2."

"Is that what you said, God?" I asked out loud. "Did you say Jeremiah 16:2?"

The impression stayed on my heart, even stronger. I reached for my Bible and thumbed through it until I found the sixteenth chapter of Jeremiah. I put my finger on the second verse and read: "Thou

shalt not take thee a wife, neither shalt thou have sons or daughters
in this place."

I leaped to my feet and ran out of the building. By the time I
reached our room I was shouting: "Glory! Hallelujah!" I burst into
the room and handed the open Bible to Dede. "Read this, Honey,
read this. God just gave it to me. He doesn't want us to stay in this
place. He wants us to move on. I don't know where or how, but
Praise the Lord anyway."

Dede sat on the side of the bed, quietly reading the verse over and
over while I paced back and forth around the room with my hands in
the air praising God. "Thank you, Jesus," she murmured. "Thank
you."

The next afternoon Dede returned from a visit to Biblical Seminary. "Guess what the Lord had me tell those folks over there," she
said. "He told me to tell them that we are going to move to Virginia
and buy a television station."

One of the manifestations of the Holy Spirit that was operative in
my life was the word of knowledge. I could tell, almost instantane-
ously, if a person was speaking truth or falsehood. As I listened to
Dede, I knew what she had spoken to the people at the seminary was
truth, God's truth. A great peace descended over me. I didn't know
how it was to take place, but more and more God was pouring out
his assurance that he was about to bring something to pass.

That night I prayed again, "Lord, this television station is there,
and I don't have the money for it. It shouldn't be sitting idle. Send
some Christian down there to get it."

"I don't want some Christian to get it," God said in my heart; "I
want *you* to have it."

I knew it was the word of God, yet my faith continued to falter
and I said to Dede, "God has shut every single door without opening
any others. He won't allow me to stay here and preach on the streets.
He won't allow me to accept a church as a pastor. He won't allow us
to be missionaries. We have been waiting here long enough. Let's
pray together in the Spirit and see if we receive anything."

The big house was quiet. The children were in bed, and everyone else had gone out. We had the building to ourselves, and the two of us knelt and began to pray in the Spirit. When nothing happened, I shouted out, "God, what do you want me to do?"

Instantly the answer was impressed on my heart. "I want you to fast and pray for a week."

I turned to Dede. "God has told me to fast and pray for a week. What has he told you?"

"Pat, the strangest thing has happened," she said. "I have a strong impression to tell you to read I Chronicles 10:12. I don't know what that verse is, but I know God is speaking to me and saying read it."

Still on our knees, we reached for the Bible, and Dede fumbled through the pages until she found the scripture verse and began to read: "They arose, all the valiant men, and took away the body of Saul, and the bodies of his sons, and brought them to Jabesh, and buried their bones under the oak in Jabesh—"

"Stop," I said, dropping my head. "Are you saying that God wants me dead and buried?"

"Let me finish. There's more." Then she read the last part of the verse: ". . . and they fasted seven days."

It was like a river of peace washing over me. This was indeed the answer.

The next morning I took seven cans of fruit juice and a sleeping bag, told Dede I was not to be disturbed for any reason short of the death of one of the children, and secluded myself in the Classan Avenue Presbyterian Church next-door.

The building was usually open only on Sunday, and then just to minister to a handful of people. It was creaky, dark, and musty, but I was determined I would spend the full seven days and nights there, fasting and praying.

The first day and on into the first night I paced the floor of the sanctuary, praying and seeking God's face. Nothing happened. That night I laid out the sleeping bag on the floor of the pastor's study and went to sleep in the darkness, hearing the old building creak around me as it cooled off from the autumn sun.

The second morning of the fast I was back in the auditorium, on my face at the front of the altar. Gradually I began to feel the sustaining power of God filling me as it had often done when I had fasted before. Then, deep in my heart, I heard him speaking to me about the television ministry. "Go and possess the station. It is yours."

This time I did not question him. I knew that the time had come for me to step out in faith and possess the land, just as Joshua had gone in to possess the land that God had promised years before.

For the next five days I paced the halls, aisles, and rooms of the deserted church building in the heart of Brooklyn. All that time, God ministered to me. I read the Book of Isaiah, the Book of Matthew, and then reread them both. I prayed, "Give me love. All I need is love."

And God said, "I am not giving you love. I am giving you hope."

Then God began to give me an understanding of the progression of a Christian toward true maturity. He taught me to recognize the things which he prizes most highly. The gifts of the Spirit are certainly important, but none of them will endure. The Christian will take into eternity the fruit of the Spirit, not the gifts. Love, joy, peace, patience, gentleness, goodness, faith, meekness, self-control will endure.

But how was I to get these great virtues for myself? God continued to teach.

All of the fruits of the Spirit are actually facets of the three great Christian virtues, faith, hope, and love. I had asked God for love, but I could never have love until first I had hope.

He showed me that I had started with faith. His faith. Now my faith had been placed in a crucible. It had been mashed, pressed down. But the mashing was necessary, because the Bible says, "The trying of your faith worketh patience" (James 1:3). And what is patience but the foundation of true hope?

The Bible tells us there is a natural progression. "Patience worketh experience, and experience worketh hope" (Rom. 5:4).

For a Christian, patience is the ability to accept the will of God—to wait quietly for his leading. From this comes endurance, which is essentially the ability to accept the will of God under trying circumstances and actual persecution. As he is faced with the very worst of situations, he begins to realize that God has never left him and has never failed to provide for his needs. Slowly there arises the deep-seated conviction that God is utterly reliable—that his will is always best. This bedrock conviction is called hope. It is never gotten cheaply.

The years of preparation and waiting, Dede's rebellion, and now Classan Avenue were just part of the price I would have to pay.

Praise God, it was worth it!

Now still in the crucible, I could look only to God. My hope was in him, while every day I was relying less on myself. As he was breaking me, he was freeing me to love him and love others.

Despite all the outward problems, I knew that he would not let me down. Now he showed me what the Apostle Paul meant when he wrote, "And hope maketh not ashamed; because the love of God is showed forth in our hearts by the Holy Ghost which is given to us" (Rom. 5:5).

"Thank you, Lord!" I cried out. "Thank you for giving me hope. Thank you that soon your love will be showed forth in my heart."

That week, fasting and praying alone in the gloom and murkiness of that old church, I learned as much about the depths of Scripture as I had learned in three years in the seminary. The Holy Spirit taught me more in seven days than ordinary teachers could have taught me in seven years. I had enrolled with Christ in the school of prayer, and he shoved me through in record time, giving me a graduate course to boot.

Day after day, night after night, I wandered through the old building, my hands in the air, singing and praising God. Sometimes I was on my knees in the pastor's study. Sometimes I was on my face in the sanctuary. Sometimes I stood in the pulpit and prophesied to the empty pews. Sometimes I just walked up and down the aisles surrounded by the Spirit of God. I drank my juice sparingly and never once felt a pang of hunger, and always, surrounding me, was the deep assurance that this was the turning point in my ministry.

When I came out of the church at the end of the seventh day, there was no question that God wanted me to move—immediately. I called George Lauderdale in Norfolk and said, "George, I'm coming down. Is there some place we can stay?"

"I know a Mrs. Jean Mayo who lives here in Portsmouth," he said. "She is a retired nurse but she has a private room, a sort of prophet's chamber like the widow kept for Elijah, and you can stay with her until you find a place to live."

"All right. God has spoken to me about the television station. Tell her I'll be down day after tomorrow."

Everybody showed up to help us pack the old DeSoto the next day. We rented a five-by-seven U-Haul trailer and packed all our earthly belongings in it.

Early in the morning on the day we were to leave, we ate a sparse breakfast and started to gather on the sidewalk for our last good-byes. Just as I was leaving the house, the phone rang. It was Harald Bredesen.

"I arose early this morning, and God spoke to me and told me to give you this verse," he said. "It is a quote from Abraham, who years before had obeyed God and went out not knowing whither he went to sojourn in the land of promise. Later Abraham sent out his servant to find a bride for his son, Isaac. The servant questioned the leading of God and Abraham replied thus: 'The Lord, before whom I walk, will send his angel with thee, and prosper thy way.' "

Even as he spoke, I felt the anointing of God, and we both began praising God in the Spirit over the phone.

We gathered together on the sidewalk around the loaded car and trailer. I looked around the circle. They were my friends who had sat with me on the ash heap of despair and discouragement while we waited for God to speak: Dick and Barbara Simmons, who had opened their house and heart and been used of God to succor us in a time of need; Dick White, Alice Blair, Ruby, the former madam now radiating the beauty of Jesus Christ, the spastic couple who in spite of their infirmity had been touched by God in deep areas of personal healing, and the tall, gaunt black Jamaican whose wide simple grin displayed a mouth full of white teeth and a heart full of love.

In their company, God had lifted from me the fear that one day he might send me to minister in a slum. And greater still, in their company God had brought Dede to a point of yieldedness so that she could stand beside me as a true partner in the ministry.

We stood on the sidewalk and held hands, praying one last time together.

The seventy dollars in my pocket comprised all our earthly wealth, and as we prayed I felt the Spirit of God upon me again, and I repeated the cryptic prophecy the Lord gave: "I am sending you into a wasteland. Do not be taken up by the wasteland. Look only to me."

XI

Thank God for Soybeans

In 1959 the Tidewater area of Virginia was literally a spiritual waste-land. For years it had been in the grip of demon power. Virginia Beach was advertised as the psychic capital of the world. It was the headquarters of Edgar Cayce and the Association for Research and Enlightenment (ARE). Mediums, clairvoyants, and necromancers flocked to Virginia Beach saying the "vibrations" in the air made their work easier. These Satanic vibrations, which traverse space and time, are the communication channels to which sensitives or medi-ums must attune themselves, and Virginia Beach was renowned as the prime receiving station of the Universal Transmitter (Satan). Stories abounded of people who discovered their psychic sensitivity while visiting in the area. Spiritualist centers dotted the Norfolk, Vir-ginia Beach area. By virtue of the fact that Norfolk was one of the largest naval bases in the world, the area was rampant with sin. In the words of one reporter, "Crime, vice, venereal disease, blight: these were the hallmarks of Norfolk as the decade of the fifties dawned."

Yet as we drove down the eastern shore of Virginia, a feeling of ex-citement began to permeate the car so that on several occasions Dede and I both broke out into spontaneous praise of the Lord. I had been reading the life of George Mueller and was determined that like that great saint of the last century, I would not rely on human re-sources and would ask no funds whatsoever in establishing God's beachhead in Tidewater.

"That seventy dollars won't last us very long," Dede said as we approached the ferry that would take us across the mouth of the Chesapeake Bay. "I'm glad we have a rich Father to fall back on."

I knew she didn't mean my earthly father. First of all, he was not rich. The Senate is known as the Millionaires' Club, but my father was one of the few who lived off his salary. Furthermore, he was aghast at my present mission, which he considered my crowning folly.

As chairman of the Banking and Currency Committee, he dealt constantly with large sums and practical people. His own practicality told him I was on a fool's errand.

"Pat's taken leave of his senses," he had told Harald. "Where is he going to get the $275,000 to buy that station—and worse, the $500,000 a year to run it? Try to bring him back to his senses."

"Yes, Dede," I replied, "if we cannot trust God to meet our personal needs, how can we trust him for the needs of a television station?"

Dede smiled her agreement. She smiled a good deal these days. She was, of course, relieved to get out of New York, but more than that, we were coming into a glorious oneness of mind and spirit. This did not mean that we would never get conflicting "guidance." But when disagreements arose, we discovered that God would soon send the same word to us both if we only continued to wait on him.

We spent the first two weeks with Mrs. Jean Mayo as we looked for a place to stay. By now Dede had learned to expect God to guide in every detail. "Do you have any word from the Lord as to where we're to live?" she asked me.

"Before we left Brooklyn, the Lord gave me one word: 'Boulevard,' " I said. "Look on the map and tell me if you see any boulevards."

"Here's something called Airline Boulevard," she said; "let's look there." We drove from one end of Airline Boulevard to the other, but nothing was for rent on it.

We paused to consult the map again. "Here's a place where two boulevards intersect," Dede said. "I don't see any others."

We arrived at the intersection of the two remaining boulevards; on the corner was an apartment complex with a "for rent" sign in the front yard. It was an upstairs-downstairs apartment that could be rented furnished or unfurnished. Since the furniture would cost us an additional ten dollars a month, we decided to take it unfurnished. We moved in the week before Thanksgiving, 1959, and invited George Lauderdale and his family to celebrate Thanksgiving dinner with us. It was quite an affair.

We splurged and bought a turkey, set our trunk in the middle of the bare living-room floor, decorated it with the silver candelabra salvaged from the "great sellout" and passed out place mats. These we used to put the plates on and to sit on. It was the most thankful Thanksgiving we had ever spent.

The following Monday I tried to call Tim Bright, the owner of the defunct TV station. His accountant said he was out of the state, and he had no idea when he would return.

I was discouraged but decided to take Dede and drive across town to try to locate the station. The address we had for the station took us through an old slum area of town and down to a dead-end street at the edge of a saltwater marsh overlooking a mud-filled tidal basin. We pulled up in the dirt drive and sat in the car for a long time, just looking. The brick building was not old, but it was surrounded with knee-high weeds. Panels on the front door were rotting, and some of the windows were broken out. "Do you think God can ever do anything with a place like this?" Dede asked.

I just shook my head. I had never seen a television station before, but in my wildest imagination I never dreamed that it would look anything like this. "Remember, it's been closed down for some time," I said hopefully. "Maybe things aren't so bad inside."

I was wrong. Things were worse inside.

I got out of the car and walked around the back side of the building. Wading through the weeds I found reels of motion-picture film scattered about—their contents festooning a gaunt-looking tree. When I got to the back, I saw where vandals had broken out the window panes, jimmied the door of the equipment control room and left it hanging askew on rusty hinges.

I climbed through a broken window to get inside the studio. The entire building had been vandalized. Wading through a couple of inches of broken glass and tubes, I pushed aside the debris that had been torn from the walls and let Dede in the front door. At the sound of my approach, a wharf rat, as big as a small cat, ran out of the building toward the nearby creek.

The control room was a shambles. The floor was littered with glass where vandals had snatched the tubes from the cameras and control panel and smashed them against the walls. The lens from one of the film projectors had been wrenched loose and thrown away. The ceiling of the control room had been ripped out and the fiberglass insulation pulled down and scattered all over the floor. Dede and I just stood there speechless, pushing our feet through the debris.

The studio was no better. The plate-glass window between the studio and control room had been smashed, and the floor was littered with beer cans. Someone had obviously urinated on the floor, filling the closed room with a horrible stench.

Everything spoke of utter desolation. Only the transmitter and live camera remained undamaged. Later we were to discover that the protection of God had been on the station even during the vandalism, for most of the other parts could be replaced at relatively small cost while these two, which cost a small fortune, remained intact.

But where was Tim Bright? The days were slipping by, and our money was dwindling to nothing. I was determined not to ask for money, so Dede got a weekend job at the hospital as a nurse, and George Lauderdale asked me to preach in some of the small churches in the Tidewater area.

In the first place I preached, the chairman of the committee handed me a five-dollar honorarium. The second church gave me a hearty handshake. But in the third church, one of the deacons came up to me after the service and said, "Pat, I haven't got any money to give, but I would like to help you."

"What do you do?" I responded.

"I sell farm supplies."

"Praise the Lord," I shouted. "Can you get me some soybeans?"

"For what?" he quizzed. "How do you use soybeans in television?"

"To eat," I answered.

"Who is going to eat them? Have you got animals on TV?"

"I'm going to eat them."

"You are! I don't believe it, but I'll see what I can do."

Later that week my friend appeared at my door. He led me outside and opened the trunk of his late-model Chevrolet. "Here's a seventy-pound bag of soybeans," he said. "But that farmer still doesn't believe any human being is fool enough to eat them."

"Praise the Lord," I murmured, with a little less enthusiasm than I usually mustered up.

But we did praise the Lord for soybeans. For us, they were the staff of life. At supper one night Tim began to complain, "Daddy, all we ever have is soybeans."

I took down the Bible and read to him from Numbers 11 where the children of Israel complained about the manna and God consumed them with fire. "You be quiet," I told Timmy; "this is God's manna."

He dropped his head and returned to the mush on his plate. "I think I'd rather have the manna," he muttered, "than these old soybeans."

Actually they were extremely nutritious. Dede bought some whole-wheat flour and baked whole-wheat bread. We bought a huge sack of oatmeal, which was very cheap, and someone gave us a sack of peanuts from Suffolk. Occasionally we would go on a spending spree and buy some peanut butter and bologna, which was a real treat. The first of December my mother sent us an old Virginia country ham. We couldn't help but laugh. Here we were eating country ham which was worth $3.50 a pound when we were so poor we couldn't afford bologna. We mixed it with soybeans, and it was delicious.

Small amounts of money were appearing in miraculous ways. In my preaching I announced that we had moved to the area to start a Christian television station. The church people knew we were living on faith and every so often someone would hand me five or ten dollars "for the ministry." Some mornings we would go to the mailbox and find an envelope with a few dollars in it. I spoke to a Baptist Brotherhood group, and they took up a love offering of about twenty-five dollars. Bit by bit, day by day, God was supplying our daily needs.

Yet we were no closer to our television ministry than when we left New York. "We need to ask the people to start praying for us at least," Dede suggested.

I remember Mrs. Edwards' testimony of the Lutheran pastor in Los Angeles who said, "Whenever God is going to do any kind of work, he always begins by prayer." I took the money from a love offering in a women's meeting and ordered ten thousand prayer cards printed.

"What are you going to put on them?" Dede asked. "We don't even know if the station is still for sale or not."

"We're going to claim it in faith," I said. "And I've already picked out the call letters."

So we fixed up the prayer cards saying, "Pray for WTFC (Television for Christ)" and then I listed several specific prayer requests including (1) wisdom to know how to start a TV station, (2) God's blessing in the negotiations to buy it, (3) favor with the Federal Communications Commission, (4) a nationwide ministry on radio and television tape, and others. I realized these were not just desires, but actual prophetic longings that God had placed on my heart. We spent the week before Christmas saturating the Tidewater area with the prayer cards, and by Christmas Dede and I both knew by faith, even though we could see no more by sight than we had seen before, that God was going to bring the television ministry into being.

We had a wonderful Christmas. We put the soybeans aside to eat a turkey provided by my parents. And then something else happened. God gave me a prophetic assurance in my heart that I was to relax and take a vacation over the holidays and that as soon as the holiday season was over, he would move.

The official vacation period ended January 3, 1960. At nine o'clock that morning I picked up the phone and called Mr. Bright's accountant. "I need to get in touch with Tim Bright," I said. "Do you know where he is?"

"It's strange that you should call today," the accountant said. "Mr. Bright has just arrived in town and is over at the television station."

"Praise the Lord," I shouted over the phone, hung up, and raced for the car.

Tim Bright was a middle-aged country boy from the coal-mining section of Virginia. He had come to Portsmouth and built a TV station to carry country and western programs, but had only been on the air a short time before closing down. He was inside the building, wandering around through the rubble. I pushed open the door and walked in.

"I'm Pat Robertson," I said shaking his hand. "God has sent me here to buy your television station."

"God, eh?" Bright said, scratching his chin and looking at the broken glass all over the floor. "How much is God willing to give me for it?"

"God's figure is $37,000, and the station has to be free from all debts and encumbrances."

Bright just looked at me. "We're standing on two and a half acres of downtown real estate," he said with his mountaineer drawl, "and the tower alone cost $100,000 to build. Now you're offering me $37,000 and want me to pay off all the debts and encumbrances ahead of time, is that correct?"

"That's right," I said innocently. "And besides, I want a six-month option."

"An option? You mean you want me to sign a paper promising I will sell the station to you at your price anytime during the next six months?"

"That's right," I said, "less all liabilities, plus a transfer of all equipment, real estate, and assets."

Bright wrinkled his forehead in unbelief. "And what are you going to give me for the option? How much earnest money?"

"I'm not going to give you anything for it, but God wants the option now so we can know for sure that you won't sell the station to someone else."

"I don't think I like God's way of doing business," he said with a wry grin on his face.

"Sorry," I said smiling, "but I'm simply his agent and have to take my orders from him."

"I guess you know I've turned my license back over to the FCC?" he said.

"That's all right," I said. "God will renew it for me."

"You're a strange one," Bright said, "but we'll talk it over and see what we come up with."

"One more thing," I ventured. "We're not sure this station even works. It looks like everything has been busted up, and after sitting idle this long it may not even transmit a signal."

"Seems like God should know the answer to that," Bright said. "Why don't you ask him?"

"I have," I replied, "but since I'm going to have to run the station for him, he told me to have you show me, too."

Bright grinned and nodded his head. "Looks like your boss knows a bit about business. Meet me up here tonight at eight, and I'll crank up the transmitter and prove to you that the station is still in operating order."

I was back at eight o'clock. The station was located right beside a body of water, and the humidity was always high. I knew the transmitter had been sitting idle for some months now and had built up water and condensation. However, Bright assured me that everything was in good condition, and with great fanfare he pulled the switch on the transmitter.

I jumped back as a great ball of fire burst out of the transmitter and shot up the transmission lines. The moisture had caused the high voltage to arc, and as the fire shot up the wet, corroded lines it completely melted the Teflon rings inside the transmission line.

I leaned against the side of the wall and looked at Bright. He was pale and shaken, but still confident. "It's okay," he said shakily, "just a little moisture in the transmitter. We can replace those melted parts without too much trouble. I think it's still working, though. Let's try 'er out."

He went into the control room and put on a record and a slide. "Now if you'll trot down the street and ask someone if you can peek at their television set for a minute, you'll see that we're on the air."

I walked down the street to a little restaurant and asked if they had a UHF receiver. They did, and I asked if they would mind turning to Channel 27, that we were testing the equipment at the station. They obliged, and so standing in Bowen's Grill I saw my first glimpse of Channel 27 on the air. The reception was fuzzy, but it was working, and inside I heard the voice of God saying, "See! Now I will take care of the other details, too."

That night I stayed up most of the night with my law books, drawing up the option I expected Mr. Bright to sign. At 2:00 A.M. I typed it out on my portable typewriter in the kitchen of the little apartment and finally got to bed just before dawn. The vacation was definitely over.

The next day I met Tim Bright at his accountant's office, and we drove over to the station in his car. He was stubborn, unwilling to come to any terms, yet as we talked he kept asking me about God.

"You're the son of a senator," he said. "Why don't you get your dad to buy the station."

"Because I'm working for my Heavenly Father and not my earthly father."

"God must be pretty real to you," he said.

I sat down on the edge of the desk trying not to pay attention to the papers scattered all over the floor, and began to share what had happened in my life. I gave him both barrels as I told him how I had discovered the power of God, had been baptized in the Holy Spirit, and even spoke in tongues.

"I believe everything you're saying," he said seriously. "I like Christianity, but have been turned off by Christians. I've developed a pretty bad reputation as a businessman. A lot of folks think I'm unscrupulous, but I really do love Jesus Christ in my heart, and you've touched me with what you're telling me about a God of miracles and supernatural power. Most guys like us believe that God is like that. But when I used to go to church, I'd hear some preacher say that miracles aren't for today. You're telling me they are. You're telling me God's still in the miracle-working business. And I believe you."

"What about the option?" I asked.

He shook his head. "I just can't do business like that. Let me think it over for a couple of weeks."

He was leaving that afternoon to drive up to Baltimore and offered to give me a ride back to where I had left my car. As we drove back through town, I sat in the seat beside him praying silently in the Spirit. Suddenly Tim stopped the car and looked at me.

"Pat, do I have to sign that option?"

"Yes, Tim, you've got to sign it. God wants you to."

"And $37,000 is your top figure?"

"That's the top and bottom figure," I said. "God said that was how much I was to pay you."

I kept waiting for him to ask me if I had the money in the bank, for I knew I couldn't lie to him. But he never asked. He seemed to assume that because I spoke with such confidence, I had the money in hand. And indeed *we* did, only at the present time it was in God's hands, not mine.

I pulled the option from my coat pocket, produced a pen, and handed it to him. He took one more strange look at me and hastily scrawled his name on the bottom. "Like I said," he grinned, "your Boss sure does know how to drive a business deal."

I began to praise God, and suddenly we were interrupted by a figure standing beside Tim's window. We looked up—it was a traffic cop. "Buddy, this is an illegal parking zone. I'm going to have to give you a ticket." With that he handed Tim a summons.

"Well, what do you know about that?" Tim said. "I just give God my television station, and now the government tries to take what little bit I got left."

But he was smiling.

And so was I.

XII

The Bank of Virginia
vs.
The Bank of Heaven

———
———
———

I now had the right to buy a television station at ten cents on the dollar, and I didn't even have ten cents.

The station was equipped for UHF, and when a new VHF channel had been assigned to the area, Bright had agreed to go off the air. Since there was no market for the UHF (no one could see the potential of UHF back then) he had been unable to sell the station. Actually the FCC was anxious to get UHF on the air, but without money I could do nothing.

I immediately went to work drawing up a charter. Fortunately my major in law school had been corporation law, so even though I was not a member of the bar, it didn't take much to draw up the corporation papers and file them with the State of Virginia as a nonprofit corporation.

Even here, I began to sense the hand of God in wording the charter. I wound up, in essence, saying that our primary purpose was to bring glory to Almighty God and his Son, Jesus Christ. In the light of this we intended to spread the truths of the Holy Bible by any means, *not limited* to the following . . . and then I listed the various radio and TV procedures. The charter was filed on January 11, 1960, under the name of Christian Broadcasting Network, Inc. Our first board of directors consisted of Harald Bredesen, Bob Walker (who had become a close friend since our first meeting in Washington), George Lauderdale, Dede, and me.

Two days after I filed the corporation papers, I received a cash contribution in the mail from a man in South Carolina who had heard of the station through George Lauderdale. I opened the letter and the money fell out on the table—three one-dollar bills.

Dede giggled. "Looks like you're beginning to deal in high finance. What are you going to do with it?"

"I'm going to open a bank account," I said.

"With three dollars? Where?"

"At the Bank of Virginia."

"Isn't that the big building with the glass front?" Dede said unbelieving. "Don't tell me you're going in there with three wrinkled one-dollar bills."

But I did. An hour later I was seated in the spacious and luxurious Bank of Virginia saying to the young lady at the new accounts desk, "I want to open a bank account."

"Commercial or private?" she asked, not even looking up from her work.

"Ah . . . commercial," I said, trying to sound secure.

"What's the name of your business?" she said, reaching for a file card and looking up at me over the top of her glasses.

"Christian Broadcasting Network, Inc.," I said proudly.

"And your address?" she said, neatly printing the name on the top line of the card.

"Er . . . address?" I fumbled.

She glanced up again with a slightly annoyed expression on her face. "Yes sir, your place of business."

"What about my home address?"

She pulled her glasses down on her nose and looked hard at me, noticing, I am sure, my nervousness. "Where does the . . . er" (and she glanced down at the card) "Christian Broadcasting Network,

Inc., do business? What is the address of your headquarters building?"

I tried to remember the address of the station and finally had to pull a notebook from my pocket and look it up. "Oh yes," I said beaming, "the address is 1318 Spratley Street, Portsmouth."

The woman hesitated a moment, then said, "I see," and neatly printed the address under the name of the corporation.

"Now it is customary to make an initial deposit," she said, reaching into her drawer for another form. "How much do you wish to deposit?"

I cleared my throat, put my hand in my coat pocket, and pulled out the three wrinkled dollar bills. In my mind I could hear Dede giggling. "Well, we're just getting started out," I said, "so my initial deposit will be three dollars."

She never blinked an eye. She just looked at me.

I pushed the money across the desk at her, and she slowly let her eyes drop to the three dirty, crumpled bills. "Three dollars," she said without a trace of emotion.

"Yes ma'am, three dollars." I began to mumble something about Jesus multiplying the loaves and fishes, but she had turned and inserted the card in her typewriter and with great finesse typed out my original deposit: "$3.00."

"Of course you'll need a checkbook," she said with a slight smile.

"Oh yes, a checkbook. I had almost forgotten," I said.

"That will be $6.00," she said. "Do you want to pay for it, or shall I take it out of your bank account?"

I peeked inside my billfold and saw that it was bare. All I had left was some change. "If you don't mind, would you just take it out of my account?" I said.

For the first time she smiled and reached into her drawer and withdrew a checkbook. "Thank you, Mr. Robertson," she said. "The Bank of Virginia looks forward to doing business with the . . ." (she glanced again at the card), "Christian Broadcasting Network, Inc."

I walked out of the bank with the checkbook in my hand. It was my first bank transaction, and already I was overdrawn three dollars.

"We need some newspaper publicity," I told Dede, "if we expect people to back us with prayer and finances. I'm going to drive over to the *Virginian Pilot* in Norfolk and give them the story."

"Do you have enough money to get through the tunnel going and coming?" Dede asked, looking through her change purse.

Together we came up with eighty cents—just exactly enough!

The newspaper people seemed only mildly interested in my exciting story. I told them how I was establishing a faith-oriented television station, that we were not going to have any commercials but were going to trust the Lord for all the support.

"Tell you what, Mr. Robertson," the cigar-chewing reporter said, "since you're the son of Senator Robertson we'll at least get a photograph, and then if we decide to run the story we can use up most of the space with your picture."

But the photographer was out, and no one could find a camera. "Can you come back later today and let us take your picture?" the reporter asked.

I ran my hand into my pocket and pulled out all the money I had —forty cents. That was just enough to pay my toll back to Portsmouth and not enough to bring me back later in the day. "Well," I said hastily putting the money back in my pocket, "it really won't be convenient for me to come back."

The reporter, trying to suppress a smile, said, "I'll tell you what we can do. We have an office in Portsmouth. Do you think it would be 'convenient' for you to go there and have your picture taken?"

"Yes, I think I could arrange that," I said.

"Fine. I'll call them and tell them you're coming, and we can get the picture from them later in the day."

I thanked him and hastily excused myself. When I reached the lobby, I realized I had forgotten a folder of papers and walked back into the room to get it. I interrupted the reporter and two other men who were almost convulsed in laughter.

"That just makes it more of a miracle when you make it happen," I told the Lord as I walked back into the street and bent my head against the cold wind that whipped off the Chesapeake Bay. "And anyway, I guess it would be hard for a newspaper to take a picture of faith."

Everything, it seemed, cost money. If it wasn't forty cents, it was $40,000. In fact, the station was in debt to the Radio Corporation of America for $44,000. Tim Bright had agreed to sell the station debt free, but I knew he was going to leave it up to me to do his negotiating. "You work it out with RCA," Bright told me when I called him.

"But we've agreed on $37,000, and this debt is for more than that."

"Talk them down," he said. "They'll settle for less."

But other problems intervened before I got to RCA. We moved into the month of February and Dede and I both caught the flu. Tim and Elizabeth also caught it, leaving only the baby, Gordon, active to run around the apartment causing havoc. Dede and I were both running high fevers, and for a week we took each other's temperature in the morning; whoever had the higher temperature got to stay in bed while the other got up and took care of the rest of us.

Our money supply had dropped off to almost nothing, and we were once again without food. The days dragged on, and my faith began to falter. Even though I slowly regained my health, my spirit was left drained. Perhaps it was the sickness, which I considered Satan's weapon of attack, perhaps it was our extreme poverty, or perhaps it was the unbelief on the part of most of those we talked to; but whatever it was, I reached a stage where I was ready to quit.

The first day out of the house I drove over to the station and on the way back began to pray. "Lord, if I have been wrong, if this isn't of you, then I want you to show me that I should stop. I don't believe you ever intend for your people not to pay their debts, and I'm in debt. The rent is due the tenth, and by then I will owe $250. If I can't trust you to look after my personal needs, then I can't trust you to look after the station. Therefore, if you don't give me some definite sign that you want me to stay in this ministry by the tenth of this month, I'm going to give up and turn to the practice of law."

There was no emotion in the prayer. It was just a simple commitment to God. I had promised him I would do whatever he wanted me to do, and I intended to keep that promise. But if I were in the wrong ministry, then it was senseless for me to continue.

I returned home and told Dede what I had done. "I'm going back into the business world, or I'll practice law, or I'll go into politics; but I'll not stay on here another day after the tenth unless God reveals himself to me."

Dede felt as horrible as I did, but she knew I was resolute in my decision. "If that's the way you feel about it," she said, "I'm with you. One thing is sure—we can't continue like this. We're out of money."

Harald Bredesen used to say that a man should make it as hard for God as he could and as easy on himself. In that way God would receive all the glory from whatever was done. A television ministry was so difficult that I wanted no part of it unless I was sure it was from God. Slick promotional gimmicks could never sustain us for what lay ahead, so I intended to stake the entire ministry on God's intervention. It had to be God's ministry or none.

On Monday, February 8, I got a call from Paul Morris at the Hillside Avenue Presbyterian Church in Jamaica. "Pat," he said, "for three weeks the Lord has told me to come down and visit you. I've just had a feeling you were discouraged, and I want to come down and be a blessing to you. Can I drive down tomorrow?"

"That's wonderful, Paul," I said. "I'm glad you're coming. We sure need a Christian brother to pick us up."

I hung up the phone but stood there shaking my head. "We need a lot more than that, brother, a lot more than that."

We hadn't seen Paul since we left New York in November, although he had sent us a ten-dollar contribution after the first of the year. We were now looking forward to his coming since our friendship had meant so much in New York, and I knew it would be good for Dede to see Helen.

At seven-thirty Tuesday night, February 9, Paul knocked at the door of our row house in Portsmouth. Helen and his three boys were with him, and we warmly embraced each other. Dede had finally gotten over the flu, although she was still weak, and we four adults gathered in the living room while the boys took our kids out into the kitchen to play.

"First of all," Paul said, "God has sent something to you."

Without saying another word he sat down at the little desk opposite the sofa and pulled out his checkbook. Dede and I stood, puzzled, while he wrote out a check.

I knew Paul was drawing less than $6,000 a year from the church he pastored, and they had three growing boys to feed and clothe. Yet something in my heart told me that he was God's answer to my prayer and that the check would be for $250—the amount we needed the next day.

"This isn't for the ministry," Paul said, standing up and holding out the check. "It is for you. The Lord told me you needed it, and that I should bring it to you."

I looked at the check, and a wave of disappointment swept over me. All I could see was $80, and we needed $250. Then I looked again. The decimal was after the last zero, not in between. It wasn't $80, but $8,000!

I wanted to laugh and shout, but instead I began to cry. It was a time of tears and rejoicing.

"You really must have been having some trouble down here," Paul said when he finally escaped our embrace. "The Lord has been after me for three weeks to get this down to you."

"But where did it come from?" I blurted out. "You don't have that kind of money."

"That's between me and the Lord," Paul grinned. "Let's just say it was from an inheritance. I was tempted to spread this out to two or three Christian groups, but God insisted I give the whole thing to you. And it's given without any strings attached. Use it for whatever you wish, and believe me, it makes me far happier to give it than it makes you to receive it."

"Then that makes us the two happiest people in the world," I shouted, grabbing Paul again and dancing around the room.

"No, the four happiest," Helen said as she embraced Dede. Then we all put our arms around each other to form a glorious huddle of love, joy, and praise, well watered with tears.

Later in the evening it was Helen who put the matter in perspective when she reminded us of the passage in the Book of Daniel when Daniel was praying and the angel of God could not get to him to answer his prayer because he had to spend three weeks contending with the Prince of Persia. And so it had taken Paul three weeks to get this money to us while we struggled under the load, but now the breakthrough had come, and we were praising God with every ounce of our being.

The next morning, February 10, the sun rose on one of those rare February days in Tidewater when the sky was clear, and the temperature soared to seventy-two degrees. Paul and I took the day off, played golf, stopped back by the grocery store and stocked up on groceries, and then sat down that night to a tremendous feast, rejoicing and praising God.

The next morning I called my mother in Lexington to tell her the wonderful news. I knew how hard she had been praying, for mother was a great prayer warrior.

She heard me out, and then there was a long period of silence on the phone. "Pat," she said at last, "do you remember that last letter you received from me?"

"Sure, Mother," I said. "I got it day before yesterday."

"Do you remember there was a page missing?"

"Yes, I wondered about that. What does that have to do with this?"

"On February 7, I was in prayer up here in Lexington," she said. "And I saw a vision. I've had only two other visions before. This time

I had been on my knees praying for you when I saw heaven opening. I saw you kneeling in prayer with your arms outstretched toward heaven. And as you prayed, I saw a packet of bank notes floating down out of heaven into your hands. I looked closely and saw that they were made up of large denominations. I didn't know how much money it was, I just knew it was a lot; and it was as if you were kneeling under the open windows of heaven, and God was pouring out his wealth upon you."

I heard mother's voice breaking over the phone, and I, too, was wiping away tears. She continued, "I wrote you that letter and told you about this vision. But at the last minute, just before I sealed the letter, I took out the page telling about the vision because I was afraid you'd laugh at me and think I was just a foolish old woman."

"Praise the Lord," I whispered through my tears.

"Thank you, Jesus," I heard mother reply from the other end.

XIII

A Mess of Pottage

At last we had enough funds to buy a few tubes and begin to refurbish the station, but the debt with RCA still hung heavy over our heads.

I drove up to New York to talk to the manager of their credit division, Sam Twohig. Mr. Twohig took me out to lunch and then to his office on the top floor of 30 Rockefeller Plaza. I had prayed on the way up and felt the Lord wanted me to give a clear witness concerning my part in this settlement.

"I'm simply an agent for God," I told this astute businessman as we sat down in his plush office overlooking the heart of Manhattan. "God has revealed it to me, plainly, that this station is to be put to use for his glory. It's the Lord's station and will be supported strictly by faith."

"That's interesting," Twohig said blandly. "Now what RCA wants is the $44,000 owed by Mr. Bright."

"We don't have that much money," I said. "All I have to work with is $37,000. You and Tim Bright are going to have to find your money out of that some way."

"All right," Twohig said surprisingly, "we'll negotiate. I'll meet with my advisers, but I know we will have to get at least $25,000."

I had expected him to be difficult to convince, but he had accepted my $37,000 figure as if it were safely tucked away in the Bank of Virginia, and the figure offered to compromise the debts hadn't seemed too big to me.

After leaving Twohig's office, however, I began to realize I had made a mistake. I should have struck a harder bargain rather than leaving the impression I was willing to settle for $25,000. I called him back.

"Mr. Twohig, I believe I represented the Lord very poorly in our talk this afternoon. Twenty-five thousand is too big a price to pay for these old obligations."

Twohig laughed over the phone. "Well, Mr. Robertson, since you're acting for the Lord, you go ask him for some more money. I don't think RCA will negotiate any lower."

"We'll see about that," I said kindly. "I'm going to be praying, and I think that God will change your minds."

I returned to Portsmouth, and three days later sent him a letter in which I said I had prayed about the matter and was willing to consider an offer of $22,000, which was exactly fifty cents on the dollar.

Two weeks later I received Twohig's answer. "Our committee has met, and we cannot go lower than $25,000."

"Be thankful," Dede said when I showed her the letter. "At least he's come down from $44,000 to $25,000."

"That doesn't make a bit of difference in the world," I said. We don't have $25,000 either. What I really think they should do is give it to us." But unable to negotiate any further at the present time, I went to work at the station, trying to get it in operating order.

By this time two people had come forth to help us. One was a man named Rainey West who had some electronic experience and volunteered to help with the engineering. The other was a teenage girl named Charlotte Barker who offered to help with the secretarial work. I agreed to pay them a portion of the contributions that were trickling in, but it was a very modest amount at the most, and some weeks it was nothing.

By early spring, I felt I had waited long enough on RCA, and I wrote Mr. Twohig a six-page, single-spaced letter telling him why he should *give* the equipment to Christian Broadcasting Network.

His return letter arrived a week later. "I have met with my advisers. We do not feel we can give you the equipment, but we will be open to any reasonable offer."

I wrote back, "All right, you've asked for $25,000. I'll give you ten cents on the dollar which is $2,500."

A few days later I received another letter. "We cannot afford your offer, but will settle for $11,000." That was twenty-five cents on the dollar for the original debt.

"Don't you see what God has done?" Dede exclaimed when she came to the station that afternoon, and I showed her the final letter. "He refused to allow them to accept your original offer of $22,000 so he could later allow you to clear the debt for half that amount."

This proved to be just one of the many times God kept us out of a so-called good deal (much to our anguish sometimes) because he knew a better door would be opening.

We immediately went into hard negotiations with Tim Bright, trying to arrive at a purchase contract. With the big RCA debt settled (I had sent them a check for $1,000 along with a note that said "Praise the Lord"), I offered to buy out Bright's remaining interest for $10,000 less any accrued taxes and the cost of repairing the broken equipment. We dickered back and forth and finally Bright said, "You know, I have come to the conclusion that God really is in this matter. Rather than haggle over the price, I think I will simply deed over the land, building, tower, and all my equity in the equipment— for nothing. You can then take care of the debts and taxes." Again God had closed the door on our original offer, so we could receive the station as a gift. It was the first of May, 1960.

Before we left New York I had received a Scripture prophecy which I never had understood, although I knew it applied to the TV station. The Scripture was I Kings 6:37. "In the fourth year was the foundation of the house of the Lord laid, in the month Zif." Now as I remembered, the month of Zif on the Jewish calendar was the month of May. The foundations had at last been secured, and prophecy was fulfilled. Four years had gone by since I had given my life to Jesus Christ.

Immediately, good things began to happen. The manager of a local FM radio station, WYFI, stopped by the station. "What's the height of your tower?" he asked.

"The original tower is 280 feet," I said, "and the extension gives it an overall height of 415 feet."

"That is what I hoped," he said excitedly. "We need a higher tower, and rather than build one, we would like to rent space on yours."

"What do you have in mind as a financial proposal?" I asked.

The man hesitated and then said, "We'd like to work out a deal with you. We are making plans to relocate our present station with new equipment. Until then, we want to run a line from our present station to your antenna. We will pay you $100 a month rent."

I could hardly contain my excitement. This was as much money as we were picking up in donations. The man quickly continued. "I know this isn't much; however, if you'll agree to a long-term lease, we'll turn over as part of the rent our entire present facilities, including all the broadcasting equipment."

It was a beautiful arrangement. They needed our tower to expand their signal. We needed the cash, and later when their new station was finished, we would be the owners of an operating FM radio station.

We shook hands, and the next day signed the contract. Our rental income would amount to $6,000, and the station equipment was worth $7,200, meaning we were getting a total of $13,000 which was $3,000 more than we still owed RCA. Even though the money was not in hand, I could see how God was showing me that he could provide all our needs.

However, we still needed a commitment for $31,000 to show the FCC that we had the wherewithal to put the station on the air. Without it, it was impossible to obtain the license.

Dede and I prayed. I called our board members, Bob Walker, Harald Bredesen, and George Lauderdale, and asked them to pray. We knew it had to come from God. It seemed the last big hurdle to cross before going on the air.

Our station property was located on the waterfront overlooking an estuary of the Chesapeake Bay. Behind the station was a boat slip, which was unused at the time. In the early summer I received a visit from a man named Tom Dangler° who had a business near the station. He was interested in renting our boat slip to dock his new boat. As we chatted, it turned out he had an interest in the Lord's work; in fact, it seemed he was extremely wealthy and was looking for someplace to invest his money to the glory of God.

My heart began to beat faster as I sensed this man might be the answer to our prayer. He asked if he could come back and talk again, and I assured him that I would be delighted to talk with him, especially since I felt we might have just the right kind of needs to meet his desire to invest money.

Over the next several weeks, we talked many times. "You know, Pat," he finally told me, "I love God with all my heart. I want to give everything I have to Jesus. I am filled with the Spirit and believe in the Full-Gospel message. I've got 140 acres out in the country that is worth $2,000 an acre, and I want to make my money work for God. You say you need $31,000. Tell you what I'm going to do. I'll purchase your property from you for $31,000 and then lease it back to you at a dollar a year for twenty years."

"Praise God!"

"Not only that," he said, as he put his arm around my shoulders, "but it will make me a partner with the greatest Christian I've ever met. I can't think of a higher honor than standing beside you in the ministry."

I went home that night walking on clouds. Dede listened as I related our conversation, but she made no comment until dinner was over and the children were in bed. We walked outside in the darkening twilight and sat on the wooden steps at the front of the apart-

° Name fictitious; events real.

ment. Two blocks away we could hear the muffled sound of the traffic on the busy thoroughfare, and someplace out in the harbor the eerie moan of a ship's horn rolled across the water. The warm breeze brought the soft smell of gardenias, and we sat and talked.

"Pat," Dede said slowly, "there's something about this that doesn't sound right."

"Honey, I know it means I'll have to go into partnership with Dangler, but how else can we raise the money?"

"It's not just the partnership," she said as she tilted her head back. "This man is going to wind up owning the entire station and everything in it."

"Dede, when you don't have anything, you can't afford to look into the future. We have to step out on faith day by day."

"Are you sure this is faith?" Dede asked. "Or is it desperation? You may get the money, but this man's going to wind up ahead. You'll have no freedom at all," she paused. "Pat, this is Satan's trap to destroy us."

"How can you say that?" I said. "We've prayed and trusted God; now this offer has come along. We won't even *have* a station unless we get some money. If Dangler puts up the money, it won't cost us anything for the next twenty years. I don't think it's all that bad a deal."

I felt Dede stiffen as I put my arm around her shoulder. "You're so dead set on this, you won't listen to reason," she said, pushing me away. "I know you think a woman is supposed to submit herself to her husband, and I believe that too. But there are times when God talks to me, too, and this is one of them. You're just like Esau, selling your birthright for a mess of pottage simply because you are hungry and willing to grab the first morsel dangled before you. This is a velvet trap to destroy Christian Broadcasting."

I felt my temper rising. I should have discerned this as a sign that something was spiritually wrong, but I had already made up my mind.

Even though Dede's words still echoed through my mind, the next day I signed the contract with Mr. Dangler. He agreed to loan us the money completely secured by all the property. It was a poor arrangement, but at last I was able to apply for our FCC license, the final step before going on the air.

Things moved like clockwork, and I soon forgot Dede's warning. The man in charge of the television branch of the FCC was a Jew named Martin Levy. Not realizing that department chiefs aren't supposed to offer legal assistance, I walked into his office and said, "I don't know very much about FCC forms. Would you mind helping me fill this thing out?"

"The government is extremely anxious to get more UHF stations on the air," he said, as he cleared his desk and motioned me to sit down beside him. "First of all, I suggest that you copy some of the material that is already on file, which will save you having to prepare it yourself."

After showing me many of the angles he said, "Now with your legal background, I think you can fill out the rest. There is a good bit of technical engineering data that you will need assistance with, however, so if you don't mind I'll call in our chief engineer, Harold Kelley, and let him show you what to do."

Picking up the phone, he dialed Mr. Kelley's office. "He's a Roman Catholic," Levy grinned, "but I figure you're going to need all the help you can get on this thing."

With the invaluable advice of Kelley and Levy as a start, the rest was easy. Finally the application was ready to be presented. "I guess you realize," Levy said, "this is the first application in the history of the FCC for a new television station that is going to broadcast 50 percent or more religious programs. I wish you the best."

Levy promised to give the application his full attention and said he would let me know as soon as the Commission had reached a decision.

I waited two months, and October was almost over. We heard nothing. Finally I put in a call to the FCC in Washington. "Mr. Levy, what has happened to our application?"

"It doesn't look like you've got enough money to put this station on the air," he said. "But the Commission figures you've got it down there somewhere, so we are going to grant you the license. We'll send you official notification in about a week."

But it was the newspapers that got the notification first. A week later, in November, the phone rang at home early one morning. It was a reporter from the Norfolk paper saying, "We've just received a teletype bulletin from the FCC that you've been granted a television station."

"Praise the Lord!" I shouted over the phone. And that was the lead on the front-page story that appeared in the Norfolk paper: Praise the Lord!

But in my excitement, I moved ahead of God, and before I realized it, I had made a couple of inaccurate statements to the papers. The most disastrous was that we were going to be on the air by Christmas. I also told the newspaper that our call letters were going to be WTFC—Television for Christ. Both statements were wrong.

"You should have checked with us before you announced your call letters," the FCC said, when I called. "Unfortunately WTFC is already assigned to the government."

This was a humiliating blow, because all our prior publicity, starting with the prayer cards, had carried the call letters WTFC. Now I was forced to go back to my supporters and tell them I had erred and run ahead of God's plan. It looked bad, because once you admit a mistake in the area of guidance, it indicates you are prone to make others. I had already made several.

Then came the final blow. Harald Bredesen had come down to spend Thanksgiving with us. It was supposed to be a time of great rejoicing, but try as hard as I could, I was unable to shake the dread feeling of impending doom.

Thanksgiving afternoon we had gathered at the station. Suddenly Mr. Dangler walked in. "Who put up those partitions in the control room?" he asked, his voice quivering.

I was speechless. He looked at me, his lips white with rage. "If I'm going to put up the money on this place, I want to know what's going on around here. Who authorized those partitions?"

My mouth grew dry, and I felt the hair on the back of my neck begin to prickle. I tried to speak, but my voice was cracked. "We needed an audio booth. Why should we have to contact you ahead of time for something like that?"

"If I own this building you won't be able to place a single board without my permission."

"Mr. Dangler, we can't do business like that," I said.

"Then I'm not going to put up any money for you."

"But we have a contract."

"Then tear it up. You've deceived me, and that constitutes a breach of contract. I will not do business with you." Turning sharply, he walked out and slammed the door.

"That man is demon possessed," Harald said. "How in the world did you get involved with him?"

I looked at Dede, but she had simply turned and walked into the darkened studio.

"Praise the Lord, Honey," she said when I walked in beside her. "Working with that man would have been the most excruciating straitjacket imaginable. God has delivered you from a bondage far worse than poverty."

"But I didn't deceive him, he deceived me."

"I realize that. But don't you see, he never had any intention of putting up any money. He was just leading you on, hoping you would go broke, and then he could take over the station and property. When God granted you the FCC license, Dangler panicked and came storming in here knowing the only way he could back out of his contract was to attack you. Pat," Dede said, turning and putting her arms on my shoulders, her forehead reaching up and just touching mine, "God wants this station run on prayer—and nickel and dime support. If you had received that big sum, not only would you have been bound to Mr. Dangler, but it would have shut off the prayer and financial support you need so badly from the thousands of people in this area. Remember, Pat, we're supposed to be walking by faith and not by sight. Always."

Dede was right. But now we were back where we started from. We did have our FCC license, but I owed RCA $10,000 and it was impossible to buy the new equipment we needed to go on the air by Christmas. We were so close, yet so far, and this time I could see where we had literally played out every potential source of income. I was finally at the point of admitting that it is one thing to say, "I believe God *can* provide," and quite another to say, "I believe God *will* provide."

XIV

A Repentant Procrastinator

―――
―――
―――

"Pat," Dede said one Sunday morning, "regardless of what happens to the television ministry, I think we need to get settled in a local church."

Dede was right. We had made some close friends in the neighborhood Baptist church. In fact, the man who had provided the soybeans was a member there. Only two months before, this church had extended to us the rent-free use of a roomy old house standing on a piece of land which they had recently purchased for future expansion. We applied to the pastor for membership, but we ran into a problem. We were told we first had to attend a six-week membership-training class.

"Sometimes I'm out preaching and won't be able to attend all the sessions," I told the pastor.

"I'm sorry," he said, "but this is church policy. Most of the people who want to join know absolutely nothing about our doctrine and procedure."

"But I've been a Baptist most of my life, long before I was a Christian," I said. "And I'm a graduate of the seminary."

"If we make an exception for one, we'd have to make it for all."

I told him I would try, but something didn't seem right about the entire matter.

However, it wasn't my inability to attend all the classes that caused the big problem; it was a far more explosive matter. I was sitting in my office at the station one afternoon when the pastor knocked at the door. His face was drawn, and he kept nervously licking his lips.

"Is anybody else here?" he asked, clearing his throat. "I'd like to talk to you privately."

"I think we're alone," I said, getting up to shake his hand.

"Are you sure?" he said, ignoring my hand as he looked out in the hall.

"I'm sure."

He shut the door while I sat back down behind my battered desk. I waited for him to speak, but could see that he was having difficulty forming the words. Finally he blurted out, "I hear that you speak in tongues."

Dede and I had agreed, before coming to Portsmouth, that we would not make an issue of our baptism in the Holy Spirit. Because of this, we had not made any public mention of our experience, although on a number of occasions we had been led to share privately with others. But not being ashamed of what Jesus had done for me, I answered, "That's right. I have spoken in tongues for several years now."

Pulling out his Bible, the pastor continued, with just a trace of hostility in his voice, "My Bible says 'whether there be tongues, they shall cease . . . for when that which is perfect is come, that which is in part shall be done away.' The Bible was the perfect thing which came into this earth, and when it came, tongues passed away. They are not for today."

This was not the first rejection of the supernatural power of God that I had run into, but I was, nonetheless, taken aback. However, the Holy Spirit is equal to all occasions, and I found myself answering, "Now brother, I don't want to be argumentative about this matter. I've never made an issue of this and don't expect to; but that's just poor exegesis. That same passage from I Corinthians 13 says 'whether there be knowledge, it shall vanish away.' If tongues are not for today, then neither is knowledge. That passage refers to the second coming of Jesus, and no scholarly exegete will say otherwise."

He gulped and began flipping through his Bible. "But . . ."

I interrupted, saying, "Besides, Paul says, 'but forbid not to speak with tongues.' "

"But that was for the apostolic age," he said, his face slowly changing from white to red and the cords in his neck beginning to bulge around his collar.

"Acts 2:39 says, 'For the promise is unto you, and to your children, and to all that are afar off, even as many as the Lord our God shall call,' " I said calmly.

"I was afraid you were this kind of person," the pastor said, standing stiffly in front of his chair. "You've been applying for membership in our church, but we cannot let you in unless you agree you will not preach or teach any of these things."

"Brother," I said, rising to my feet behind the desk, "I can't restrict the Holy Spirit. I can't agree not to teach certain important parts of the Bible just because you don't believe them or understand them. I don't know whether the Lord would ever tell me to teach about tongues, or even to speak in tongues in one of your meetings, but I do know that it would be wrong for me to deny that these things are so, or to promise to quench the Spirit in my life. That is in direct opposition to the teachings of that Book you hold in your hand."

"Well, if that's the case, we can't accept you or your family as members of our church." Without another word, he turned and walked out.

"Oh God," I breathed, slumping back in my chair, "now what's happened? I didn't think things could get any worse, and now even my church has excluded me—simply because I trust in you and believe your Word to be true. I don't know how much more I can take, God. I just don't."

I felt like Adlai Stevenson when he was defeated for the presidency in 1952 and talked about the little boy who stubbed his toe and was too little for it not to hurt and too big to cry. I felt a strange lump in my throat and a heavy weight settling on my heart.

Within a week, the oppression seemed to descend upon me from all sides. Our engineer quit. I thought it was because there was no money coming in to pay his salary, but our secretary said he had told her he was disgusted with all that "prophecy and stuff."

Knowing the fullness of the Spirit, I had begun to be free in our little staff prayer meetings, but I guess I was too free. Now I found myself choking up inside even when I tried to pray alone. If I had a message in the Spirit, I was afraid to bring it forth. Suddenly I felt horribly bottled up.

It didn't stop there. I had been invited to speak to a group of local ministers at a luncheon meeting. Feeling this was a chance to garner their support, I shared my dreams about reaching Tidewater with Christian television. They sat patiently while I poured out my heart and challenged them to join me in this tremendous outreach throughout the Tidewater area.

After I finished speaking, I was called from the room to answer the telephone. I returned just in time to hear one of the leading Methodist ministers comment, "Well, if we can't stop it, at least we can dissociate ourselves from it."

I didn't even have the heart to reenter the room. I just walked out the door and drove slowly across the city to our house.

As soon as I walked through the doorway, Dede knew something was wrong. "Pat, what happened today."

"Honey, it wasn't just today," I said, my voice choking. "Look at all that's been happening. I can't take anymore."

"Do you mean the problem with the church?" she asked, as I slouched into the big armchair.

"I wish that were the only thing wrong," I replied solemnly. "Don't you see the mess we're in? Dangler broke his word, and now we owe thousands of dollars. Our one engineer has walked out. Most of the fundamental churches are turning against us because of our experience with the Holy Spirit, and just today I got the kiss of death from the liberals. Can you imagine what a laugh the rest of the town is going to have when they learn that the *faith* television station went bankrupt?"

Dede walked over to where I was sitting. She knelt beside me. "Darling, we are no worse off than we were in Brooklyn."

I shook my head. "We didn't owe RCA $10,000 in Brooklyn. We may have been little fools up there, but we've been big fools down here—down here in Dad's backyard."

"Pat," she said quietly, "God is still with us."

"That's just the problem!" I exploded. "For years I've tried to do God's will. Now everything is wrong. I'm out on a limb and it looks like God is sawing it off. I've got to do what he wants, because he's bigger than I am, but it all seems so unfair!"

A feeling of hopelessness was settling over me as I talked. "I've staked my whole life on my belief that God works supernaturally today—that he is alive and ready to answer prayer. I thought that I was hearing his voice and that he was speaking to me out of the Bible. *Where am I going to turn if all that was wrong?*"

"Pat," Dede exclaimed, "don't you remember how God healed Timmy? If that isn't enough, think about Paul Morris and the $8,000."

Somehow her words fell on deaf ears. Up to that time I had been proud that we had been living on faith like George Mueller. I had boasted that we were going to rely solely on God for everything. Now a few swift blows had made a shambles of my vaunted faith, and to my shame, I had actually questioned the goodness of God.

"I am going to sell the station and pay our bills," I said matter-of-factly. There was nothing more to say.

Two things happened to persuade me that my decision to get out of the television ministry was correct. The first was a phone call from Mrs. W. L. Lumpkin, the wife of the pastor of the big Freemason Street Baptist Church in downtown Norfolk. Dr. Lumpkin, her husband, had been pastor of the Manley Memorial Baptist Church in Lexington when I was a youngster. During that time Mrs. Lumpkin had led my mother to the Lord, and from that experience had sprung a close friendship. She said their church was having a youth retreat at the Baptist Conference Grounds at Eagle Eyrie and wanted me to come as the featured speaker. I accepted, and we had a great weekend with the young people. Many of them came to know Jesus Christ as their personal Savior.

When we returned to Norfolk, Mrs. Lumpkin called again. "I have talked to my husband about this," she said, "and we're wondering if you would be interested in being the Minister of Education at our church."

Dede and I prayed, but we seemingly had no choice. We had no income from any other source (other than Dede's weekend wages from nursing), so out of financial necessity I accepted the offer. Again Dede's insight proved correct. We had been rejected at a small church so we could be accepted at a much larger one—with a salary of (Praise the Lord) $100 a week.

It was a wonderful experience, not only because I was getting paid regularly, but because these people were some of the finest and most gracious people I had ever met. The first thing I did was have a long talk with Pastor Lumpkin.

"You need to know my beliefs," I said. "I believe in the supernatural experience of the Holy Spirit, and that God still works miracles today. I also believe in and practice the gifts of the Holy Spirit as a personal experience."

Dr. Lumpkin, one of the great scholars of the Southern Baptist Convention, looked at me and then said with deliberation, "I believe the same thing, Pat."

At last I knew I was where God wanted me.

The second factor that pointed me away from the television ministry was an unexpected and unsolicited offer to buy us out. I was approached by the Norfolk School Board with an offer to buy the station to establish an educational television station. They were prepared to pay me $35,000 for my interest. This would allow me to pay off our debt to RCA and still come out with a $25,000 profit. I would be able to go off to sit in the sun on a Florida beach and lick my wounds. After that, there would be money available for another worthwhile effort. My mind was telling me that God's will had changed and that he wanted me to leave the TV dream and devote my full time to the institutional church. My heart was crying out for a better answer, but since none came, I took steps to secure the approval of the Board of Directors for the proposed sale.

I called Harald Bredesen on the phone, and he told me that he was getting ready to come to Washington to attend a regional convention of a group known as the Full Gospel Business Men's Fellowship International. "These are Spirit-filled men from all denominations," Harald said. "Demos Shakarian is the president, and they'll be meeting at the Continental Hotel. Why don't you, Dede, and George Lauderdale drive up? Bob Walker and I can meet you, and we can hold our board meeting and attend the convention at the same time."

It was a good suggestion, and the third week in February I took off a few days from my work at the church and we drove to Washington.

I told the board my problems—and my decision. "I kept thinking that God was going to work a miracle. But he hasn't done it. I really thought I understood the life of faith, and I've really tried to live it—like George Mueller did—trusting God and never asking for anything. But it just doesn't work—not for me anyway. We're not just broke—we're deep in a hole. I want out, and this deal with the school board is the way to let me out. All I need is your approval."

Harald Bredesen was the first one to speak up. "Pat, there's a lot more involved than whether you're broke and hungry. We've all been praying about this matter, and I, for one, am opposed to selling. I think we should hang on to the vision and stick it out."

"Now wait a minute," I argued, never expecting to run into this kind of opposition. "You guys aren't in the position I'm in. I've exhausted every resource. There's just no more money to be had. I've waited and fasted and prayed, and it's as though God has turned off his blessings. I want out, and if you guys won't sell, then I'll go ahead and sell it myself."

"You can't do that, Pat," Bob Walker joined in. "We're a corporation. You can't sell on your own motion, and we don't think God wants us to sell."

"Pat," Harald said, "you and Dede are too close to this thing to see what God is doing. But from where we are standing, it's quite clear."

"What's clear?"

"God is showing you your pride, so he can deal with it."

"Pride!" I exploded. "What do I have to be proud about? I'm broke. Hungry. Disgusted. Thousands of dollars in debt. Cast out of my church. Ridiculed by reporters and ministers and humiliated in public because of my blunders. Now you have the audacity to say I'm proud."

Harald waited until I calmed down and then continued. "Pat, you're simply proving what I'm saying. You're proud of the fact that you've lived like George Mueller and never asked anyone for money. You're proud of the fact that you're in a position where if God doesn't do it through you, it just won't get done. But now God is humbling—"

I didn't let him complete the sentence. "If I'm all that proud, maybe I'm not the guy to do—"

"Don't say that," Harald broke in. "God knew what he was doing when he picked you, but he's not going to use you until you die to an awful lot that you are alive to now."

"What are you talking about?" I snapped.

"I'll tell you what I'm talking about: your image of yourself as a man of faith. You are too proud to ask anybody for help. And there's something else, dear brother. You are afraid that people will think you're a religious fanatic, so you have been sitting on your testimony. Sure, when you are cornered, you will come out with it—but only when you are cornered. And I'll tell you something else, Pat. You hate to admit you have ever made a mistake. Remember those call letters? It practically killed you to admit you had been wrong."

Harald was being brutal, but my spirit agreed with every word. These were the wounds of a friend.

"Pat, dear brother, I've got to go on. You have got to die to your desire to vindicate yourself. You have had a personal stake in getting this station on the air, besides God's glory. All the time you have had one eye on those who have been laughing at you, your professors at Biblical, your father and brother, those ministers down in Tidewater —you've had one eye on them and one eye on God. I repeat, Pat, you are God's man for this television ministry, but first God had to purify your motives. Now that you are willing to have it known that you are a failure and shut the door on the whole project, God can begin to use you."

"Harald," it was Bob Walker speaking, "a moment ago you spoke of what Pat had at stake in the success of this project. I wonder if we fully realize what God has at stake here. It is something far more significant than getting a television station on the air, important as that is. *God's* reputation, *his* name is at stake."

We were all silent. Bob's deep voice seemed to add special emphasis to every word. He continued, "Does God answer prayer or doesn't he? Does God really do miracles or doesn't he? Sure, Pat's motives may not have been 100 percent pure. Whose are? But Pat, as much as any man I have ever known, has sought to hear the voice of God and be led by him. He has staked his whole life and his family's, too, on his conviction that a man who really wants to hear from God and be led by God at whatever cost can indeed hear from God and be led by him."

"That's right," Harald exclaimed. "God isn't building just a television station. He is building a testimony to the kind of God he is. This isn't the end. This is the beginning."

By this time both George Lauderdale and Dede were nodding their heads in agreement. "Then what are we going to do?" I said.

"I've got to raise a minimum of $10,000 or be in the absurd position of having a 'faith' ministry file bankruptcy."

"It's almost midnight," Harald said, glancing at his watch, "but let's go up to Demos Shakarian's room. I know he's still up. Demos is a wealthy dairyman; maybe if we let him know our problem, he'll want to make an investment."

Harald was right about Demos still being up. But he was wrong if he thought he would be willing to talk about making an investment. All Demos was interested in talking about was cows, which didn't seem to be the answer at all. (He later told me that was all the Lord told him to talk about.) So, we were still right where we had been.

The next day was Saturday. After lunch, Dede came up and handed me a newspaper. "Someone from Norfolk drove up today. He brought me this copy of the morning paper."

I opened it to where she indicated and saw a letter-to-the-editor. It said, in essence, "The Christians of Tidewater have just missed their greatest opportunity. For more than a year, Pat Robertson, son of Senator A. Willis Robertson, has been trying to open a Christian television station in our area. He has received almost no support from the Christians and churches. Now through lack of interest, vision, and initiative on the part of the people, the opportunity has almost fallen through. Pat Robertson is going to sell the station, and the vision will be forgotten."

"Thank you, Lord," I breathed. "But letters to the editor aren't enough. It's going to take money—and lots of it."

That afternoon I attended my first Full Gospel Business Men's Fellowship meeting. Demos was leading, but my spirit was not in tune with the meeting. The burden was still there. The debt was still there. The recognition of failure was still there, as well as the sting of Harald's rebuke of the night before. Yet as the service progressed, I gradually became aware that I was sitting in the midst of a thousand Spirit-filled people, just like myself. And everyone but me was praising God. I looked around, and the room was filled with the praise of God. Everyplace I looked, I saw men and women with their hands raised in the air. I had seen this in small meetings, but never with such a great crowd.

Almost automatically I raised first one hand, then the other, and my lips began to speak praises to Jesus. Suddenly I was praying in the Spirit, worshiping God, and pouring out love and adoration for my Heavenly Father. And at that moment, as clear as any human voice I have ever heard, I heard Jesus' voice speak in my mind, saying, *"This is my work. I'll carry the burden."*

That's all he said. But it was enough. The great stone that had been sitting on top of my heart rolled away, and the resurrection power poured from my innermost being like a river of living water. The burden was gone, replaced by faith. Hallelujah!

Following the service, someone grabbed my arm. "You have a telegram waiting for you at the front desk."

It was an anonymous wire from Norfolk. It said, "Oh, you who have labored and struggled to do something for God in this community, take heart. We are with you. I am going to help in every way I can, and am starting by making an immediate pledge of $500 toward your work. Please don't sell the station. I shall contact you when you get home."

It was signed, "A Repentant Procrastinator."

I returned to Tidewater a different man. The outward circumstances seemed to be the same, but I knew that Jesus was going to work out the circumstances. He didn't waste any time.

Monday, after we returned to Norfolk, the repentant procrastinator called me at my office. Not only did he bring me a check for $500 but he introduced me to a typesetter. The typesetter introduced me to a printer, and together they introduced me to the Camp Paper Company in Franklin, which donated paper so we could print up a tabloid newspaper. We distributed it all over Tidewater. The bold banner headline read: "GOD'S DECISION: NO SALE."

XV

On the Air

———
———
———

As I began applying myself to my new job as Minister of Education at the Freemason Street Baptist Church, I slowly realized my entire concept of "the ministry" had changed. The Apostle Paul worked as a tentmaker in order to support himself so he could preach. I had always thought the modern counterpart was the man who held a secular job so he could afford to minister in a church that couldn't pay a living wage. Now I found myself in a reverse role. I was working at a church to support myself so I could minister through the television station. It was quite a switch, but I'm not sure it wasn't a much closer parallel to Paul's ministry than I actually realized.

A month after I returned from Washington, a young man walked into my office at the church and said, "I'm a first-class licensed television engineer who's recently been baptized in the Holy Spirit. Could you use me at your station?"

I usually didn't get exuberant in the church office, but this time I came leaping out of my chair, shouting, *"Hallelujah!"*

His name was Harvey Waff, and he was getting ready to graduate from the Norfolk Division of William and Mary College. He volunteered to help us until he was out of school, at which time, I promised him, I would trust God to raise enough money to pay him some kind of salary.

Like most Spirit-baptized people I had met, Harvey was not motivated by the love of money. "All I'll need is enough to live on," he said. "What I really want to do is serve the Lord and be recompensed by his grace."

In July, Dede and I left our children with friends in the church and drove to Miami Beach to attend the national convention of the FGBMFI. Demos Shakarian introduced me from the platform and asked the thousands of people there to pray for our ministry. I returned to my seat with the confidence that nothing could hold us back now that we had all these prayer warriors behind us.

As I reached my seat, a young man came down the aisle and tapped me on the shoulder. "May I speak to you for a moment?" he said.

Kneeling in the aisle beside my seat, he introduced himself as Neil Eskelin, stating that he had a master's degree from Ohio State University in Radio and Television Programming and was filled with the Holy Spirit.

"Brother," I whispered, so as not to disturb the others around us, "would you like to come and work with the Lord in Portsmouth? I can't promise you a salary, but I'll promise you a nice office."

He grinned and squeezed my arm. "I didn't come to ask for a job, Mr. Robertson. I just wanted to let you know who I am and that like all these other folks, I'll be praying for you."

But I felt God had a far greater purpose for Neil than for him to pray for us. Three days later, as we headed north in our car, Dede and I discussed Neil Eskelin. Driving north out of Jacksonville, we came to the St. Mary's River, the boundary between Florida and Georgia. "Before we leave this state, I want to stop and pray," I said.

Dede nodded, and we pulled off U.S. 1 beside the picturesque river that wound its way slowly between the ancient oaks that overhung the banks. I sat quietly, watching the brown water swirl around the stumps and exposed roots on the bank, flowing toward the sea. It reflected the overhanging trees with the Spanish moss reaching down and softly caressing the surface, and I sensed the soft touch of the Holy Spirit on my life. I prayed, "Lord, we claim this boy, Neil Eskelin, for your ministry. In Jesus' name, Amen."

We started the car, crossed the river, and drove north through Georgia and the Carolinas to Virginia.

Exactly one week later, early one evening there was a knock on our apartment door. There stood Neil Eskelin with his suitcase. "I'm ready to start to work for Jesus," he said.

We celebrated Thanksgiving in July that year.

Our staff began to shape up. We had Harvey Waff, first-class licensed engineer; Neil Eskelin with a master's in radio and TV programming; several volunteer people who came in to help us with whatever needed to be done; a young lady named Shirley Jones who worked as a stenographer and played the piano; and me, who had never been in television.

The first Saturday morning in September, I called Harvey and Neil into my office to share something God had told me the night before. "Before you get started," Neil broke in, "I've got to say something. I came up here thinking I knew how to set up the programming for this station. But I've not been able to get any spiritual freedom in what I'm doing. Now I'm having to admit I know absolutely nothing about programming a Holy Spirit directed television station. Last night God said, 'All right, Neil, you've done it your way, now I'm going to do it my way.' I just wanted you all to know I've taken hands off all the programming and am going to let the Holy Spirit direct it."

"Wonderful!" I exclaimed. "Now we're getting somewhere. This confirms what I was going to tell you. Last night the Lord spoke to me also. He told me to announce, on faith, that we're going on the air October 1."

"We'll never make it, Pat," Harvey said, shaking his head. "You can't imagine the condition of that old equipment. We need thousands of dollars for tubes, and half the stuff is corroded from all this salt air. If we get on the air by the first of the year we'll be lucky."

"There's no luck when you're directed by the Holy Spirit. Do the best you can. Splice wires, exchange tubes, beg and borrow what you can, and trust the Lord to provide funds for the rest. But God has given me the date of October 1, and I believe he will keep it."

"I'll try," Harvey said, "but even if I work up here twenty-four hours a day, I can never get this stuff ready by then. It's physically impossible."

Harvey Waff wasn't the only one who said we couldn't go on the air October 1; so did RCA in New York. I had no sooner made my announcement than I received a wire from their credit department. "Anticipate receipt of $10,000 under contract prior to commencement of first broadcast."

"We'll just have to trust God for this, too," I told Dede. "If he wants the station on the air, he'll have to provide the money."

"Praise the Lord," she said, squeezing my hand and wrinkling her nose. "Now you're talking like the old Pat."

There were two other things that needed to be done. The first was to change our call letters.

At breakfast one morning I opened my Bible to the Book of Jeremiah, out of which God had spoken so many times. Poring over the 15th chapter, my eyes were riveted on verse 16: "Thy words were found, and I did eat them; and thy word was unto me the joy and rejoicing of mine heart; for I am called by thy name, O Lord God of hosts."

Then Bob Walker's words flashed across my mind: "God's reputation, his name, is at stake."

"Dede," I called out, "I've got it!"

"Got what?"

"The name for the station. If God's name is at stake in this ministry, then let's name it after God."

"Do you mean WGOD?" she laughed.

"No, not the English name, but the Hebrew. The sacred covenant name for God in the Old Testament is YAHWEH. It means 'He who causes everything to be.' We could call the station WYAH-TV. Then we would truly be called by his name."

She looked up, and a smile spread across her face. "This is from God. Do you remember those old call letters?"

"How could I ever forget?" I moaned. "WTFC-TV, Television For Christ."

"When we were putting on a television station *for* Christ, we didn't get very far, did we? Pat, I don't believe that we can ever do anything *for* him. Unless he does it, with or without us, it won't be done. Every time we see these new call letters, we can remember whose station this really is."

I laughed. "Then we shouldn't have any trouble clearing these call letters with the FCC." In a matter of weeks, the clearance came, and we became the first television station ever to be called by God's name.

The other matter that needed settling was approval for our radio license on the FM station we were ready to take over. We filed for the license and were granted an FM permit to broadcast on 104.5 mc, using the old equipment we had taken in on trade for rental space on the tower.

But the thing we needed most, the $10,000 to pay off RCA, was still missing. We were into the last week of September, and our promotion was going strong, saying we were going on the air Sunday afternoon, October 1. But it was all on faith. With only five days to go, and Harvey Waff working a punishing schedule and insisting we'd never make it, with RCA waiting to prevent it, and with Neil saying it would take another three weeks to complete the sets, things did indeed look dark.

Friday night, before we were to go on the air Sunday, I received a phone call from Reverend Stewart Brinsfield in Baltimore. He had heard we had obtained the license on the FM station and wanted to buy some time to broadcast.

"How would you like to buy the whole station?" I asked.

"You must need money pretty desperately," he said.

"We've got to raise $10,000 by day after tomorrow," I told him.

"How much do you want for the station?"

"I'll sell you the whole thing for $5,000."

"I'll take it," he said, "but I can't drive down to pay you until Monday."

"Okay; as long as I have your word on it, I'll go ahead. Just remember, I'm the one who's going to be sued if things don't work out."

That was half of what we needed, and we had two days to go. Saturday passed, and we spent all day at the station feverishly working on props and scenes while Harvey sweated and worked desperately over the control panel, the transmitter, and the cameras. We worked far into the night, and I finally got home in the early hours of the morning, exhausted and drained.

"We'll never make it," I told Dede, as I crawled into bed. "Harvey says it will take him another week to get things ready. He's going to go over early in the morning and try, but he says it's impossible. And besides that, we're twelve hours away from broadcast time and still $5,000 short. We might make it by November 1, but not by tomorrow."

I turned over and felt a sense of dread crushing in on top of me. Behind me, I felt Dede's warm hand gently massage the back of my neck, and then she ran her fingers through my hair. "We'll make it Pat. Remember, it was *God* who promised."

"Praise the Lord," I mumbled, knowing the words came from my lips and not from my heart.

We arose early the next morning since I still had to perform my duties at the church before I could get back over to the station. The feeling I had carried to bed with me remained as I came down for breakfast—fear, depression. We just weren't ready.

Sitting at the breakfast table, I opened my Bible to the Psalms and began to read: "Surely his salvation is nigh them that fear him; that glory may dwell in our land" (Psa. 85:9).

"Did you hear that?" I said, looking up at Dede and the three children who were sitting around the table. " 'Nigh them that fear him.' That means it is at hand. It's right here. It doesn't mean in the future. It means now. Today's the day that glory shall dwell in the land."

The burden lifted, and sitting at the breakfast table, the entire family joined in praising God for his marvelous victory. We *knew* his salvation was nigh.

We piled in the car and left for Sunday school. Driving across Portsmouth toward the tunnel, we pulled up at a stoplight, and I glanced at the man in the car beside us. It was Jim Coates, a prominent member of the Gideons, a faithful prayer supporter of the television ministry, and an official of the Norfolk Shipbuilding and Drydock Company.

"What do you suppose Jim Coates is doing all the way over here this hour of the morning?" Dede asked. "Doesn't he live over on the other side of Norfolk?"

I rolled down my window, honked my horn, and waved at him. "Hey Jim, we are going to be opening the TV station at one o'clock. I want you to come by. It will be a big event."

"I'll be there if I can," he shouted back. The light changed, and we drove off.

We arrived at church and found the people excited. "We're going to rush home right after church, Mr. Robertson," one woman said, "and put our television set on Channel 27." Another man came up to me and said, "I guess you know the most important major league baseball game of the season is being played this afternoon. But I'm going to skip it just to watch Channel 27."

"Pat," Dr. Lumpkin said, "I'm going to announce from the pulpit this morning that WYAH-TV is going on the air at one o'clock, and then I'm going to let you skip the morning worship service, since I know you have to get to the studio. God bless you. We're all praying for you."

I didn't have the heart to tell him that unless God provided $5,000 in the next two hours we'd never make it.

I rushed back over to the station. Harvey Waff was frantic, neck-deep in wires and tubes. Looking up from behind the control panel, with an electric soldering iron in his hand, he said with anguish, "I've been over here since before dawn. We'll never make it, Pat. You've missed God. You're too early. You shouldn't have set it for this date. You're wrong." With tears streaming down his face, he immersed himself in the back of the control panel again.

In the studio, Neil and several volunteers were working, desperately trying to arrange the sets. He had fashioned a crude wooden pulpit in front of a faded gray curtain that had a cardboard cross pinned on it. He had scheduled a preacher by the name of Damon Wyatt to come on the air with the first program, which was to be shared with the Branch Sisters, country hymn singers. But that didn't make any difference. None of it did. We still needed $5,000, and it was now 12:45, fifteen minutes until air time.

I walked back into my office, at the same time that Jim Coates came through the door from the parking lot. Wrinkling my brow and shaking my head, I said, "Jim, we've got a problem."

"What's that, Pat?" he said, pulling off his glasses and wiping them. "I thought you were going on the air in fifteen minutes."

Suddenly I heard that inner voice I had learned to recognize saying to me, "Ask Jim Coates."

"Lord," I argued back silently, "I've never asked anyone for money, and I'm not going to do it now, even though we're only minutes from the deadline."

"Are you still so proud that you'll not do what I tell you to do?" God said patiently. "Who knows my plans and purposes? Who are you to tell me I have to work in specified ways? *Ask Jim Coates.*"

"But Lord, you told me to live on faith. George Mueller never asked anyone for money. He just prayed, and it came in."

"*Ask Jim Coates.*"

I looked up to Jim. "Do you know anybody who's got $5,000 they'd loan us? We can't go on the air unless we have it in hand."

"Are you asking me to loan it to you?" Jim said.

"No," I said defiantly, "I just wanted to know if you knew anyone."

He thought a moment. "I know one woman down in Franklin who might do it."

"How about calling her?" I said, putting him on the spot and motioning him to the phone.

He dialed, but no one was at home. I glanced at the clock: ten minutes before one. Jim sat at my desk, his head buried in his hands —praying. I paced the floor back and forth. Then without warning Jim said, "I'll loan it to you."

"What?" I said unbelieving. "Do you have that much money available?"

"I've got some real-estate investments and some other things," he said. "I can borrow it from my bank tomorrow. The Lord has told me to do it."

I bolted from the office and went running back into the control room, shouting, "Hallelujah! We've got the money. Now put us on the air, Harvey." It was exactly one o'clock.

We didn't make it at one. But at three o'clock, October 1, 1961, Harvey threw the switch, and Neil focused the camera on me, standing in front of the cardboard cross, and we came on the air with me praying. It was my first time to appear on television.

The signal was in black and white, of course, and it was halty and shaky. Our equipment broke down twice that afternoon, and one of the films got stuck in the projector. Damon Wyatt preached, the Branch Sisters sang, and we were on a total of two and a half hours.

Surely his salvation is nigh them that fear him; that glory may dwell in our land.

XVI

"Just Hang on a Minute, Folks"

———
———
———

The phone was ringing in the office, and the secretary shouted down the hall, "It's for you, Mr. Robertson."

A woman who introduced herself as Mrs. Rockhill said, "I have been watching your television station and want you to know it is an answer to prayer."

"Yes ma'am," I said, "a lot of us have been praying for a long time for it."

"No, you don't understand what I mean. Back in the summer of 1953 a small group of us had been meeting in a Wednesday morning prayer group. We had been waiting, tarrying, seeking, and receiving. This was long before most folks knew anything about the power of the Holy Spirit. An itinerant preacher had come from Philadelphia to minister, but there had been few results. Norfolk was such a sinful place with its fleshpots and dead churches; it was as though it were Satan's seat. But the morning the minister left, he prophesied, saying, 'God is going to establish a center in this Tidewater area, and this end-time message will go out all over the eastern seaboard and spread throughout the country.'"

Mrs. Rockhill paused, and I could hear her trying to control the tears as she spoke. "We all thought it was a false prophecy at the time. We just didn't see how any good thing could come out of Tidewater. Now I realize that God knew far in advance what he was going to do."

As Mrs. Rockhill spoke, I could feel my heart beating wildly in my chest. Every cell in my body witnessed to the truth of her testimony. "In that group that morning was a dear brother I want you to meet," she continued. "His name is John Stallings. He is an ordained, Spirit-baptized minister, and is president of the Christian Deaf Fellowship of America. I feel God wants the two of you working together."

That afternoon I contacted John Stallings. It was a contact that would develop into a long and lasting ministry together.

But it was hard to see how CBN could be the center of any kind of nationwide (much less worldwide) ministry. Our one ramshackle studio room was only twenty-seven by twenty-seven and had been described by one of the local newspaper feature writers as being no bigger than an executive cloakroom. We had a few 1,000 watt spotlights dangling from the ceiling, and some of them were burned out. Our equipment was pieced together and was constantly burning out or wearing out—sometimes in the middle of a program. We were bragging about getting tubes that other stations had thrown away after putting 1,100 hours on them, and using them for another 1,000 hours—when the life expectancy was only 900 hours. We never knew from one moment to the next when we might be blown off the air.

One evening, shortly after we had begun broadcasting, we had a group of singing men standing before the camera. As they hit their loudest and highest note, the transmitter abruptly slammed off the air. Everything in the studio came to a dead silence. The one monitor set simply faded out. We were off the air.

We scurried around trying to find what had happened, and finally managed to pry open the doors behind the big transformers that carried the tremendous voltage necessary to operate the transmitter. There, caught between two electrical poles, was a tiny mouse—completely fried. We cut the power, I reached in and pulled him out, and we were back on the air again. I came before the camera and apologized to our viewers (in case there were any left), explaining that it's the little things that turn off the power. It was a good sermon object lesson, but I'm afraid most of even our faithful listeners had by that time switched us off in favor of one of the network programs.

My relationship with John Stallings had at once become a working one, and we asked him to be a part of our broadcasting team. Since John's major ministry was among the deaf, we thought it would be unique to minister to the deaf via television, something few had ever tried. We scheduled the program for eight o'clock Tuesday nights and advertised it under the title, "The Deaf Hear."

Brother Stallings arrived at the studio, and we set up his few props. Promptly at 8:00 P.M. he came on, ministering in sign language. At the close of his program, just as he was about to sign off, there was a tremendous flash of sparks and smoke in the control room, and Harvey frantically motioned me to come running. "We've just blown out a tube in the audio part of our transmission," he said anxiously. "We're still transmitting our picture, but all the sound is gone."

I ran back to the studio and tried to make signs to John Stallings to stay on the air. Realizing he didn't understand me, I grabbed a piece of cardboard and started writing him a big sign. Then it hit me. We were off the air with sound anyway, so while he continued his sign language to the camera, I shouted, "We've lost the voice part of our transmission. Can you keep going until we get it fixed?"

John grinned, nodded, and continued the rest of the night with his sign language. It was another "first" for the television industry, although I later admitted this was one time God allowed us to walk by "sight" and not by faith alone.

We didn't have video tape, so the majority of our programs were live, and it took a great deal of innovating to keep the action moving. Our sets were all built back to back, and when we changed programs, since we had only one camera, we just had to swing the camera from one set to another. Sometimes this meant "panning" all the way around the room, past two or three sets, until we could focus on the one for the next program. Neil Eskelin, who was announcing, would say into the microphone as the camera began its dizzy swing around the room, "Just hang on a minute, folks."

And hang on is what our viewers had to do. Performers were hustled into the studio and then hustled out. While one man was standing in front of the camera praying or preaching or singing, just a few feet from him another group of people would be trying to get ready for the next program. One of our most difficult tasks was to try to keep novice television performers looking at the camera, since there was so much to attract their attention in other parts of the room.

It was nothing for a man to be standing before the camera, preaching his heart out, only to see some technician crawling across the floor right in front of him trying to get to the other side of the room without being seen on the camera. Doors would bang open and closed; great gusts of wind from the outside would blow women's hair or snatch the sheet music from their hands. One night we had a distinguished preacher before the camera, and in the middle of his sermon someone opened a door and let in a great draft of air. It blew away his sermon notes, ruffled the pages of his Bible, and blew his hair on end. He bravely kept his face pointed toward the camera and continued preaching, but his eyes moved wildly in all directions as he tried to find out what was going on. Finally the door was closed with a horrible bang which vibrated through the entire studio. People were crawling around all over the floor picking up his sermon notes, trying to hand them back to him so they wouldn't be seen on camera. I just looked at Neil and moaned. "Sometimes I think we should be showing what goes on off camera rather than what's on the set—it's a lot more interesting."

One of our first program ideas was a ministry to children. Neil came up with a program called "Mr. Pingo and His Pals." Pingo was a little teddy bear that squeaked, and Neil was Cousin Neil. He played the ukulele and talked to Mr. Pingo. To liven the show, Neil decided to send Mr. Pingo scuba diving. Actually, he had positioned him behind a goldfish bowl. The cameraman shot his picture through the bowl while the fish swam in front of his face. All the while, Eric AuCoin, our seventeen-year-old audio man, was blowing bubbles with a straw into a glass of water to get the proper underwater teddy-bear sounds. The production was flawless.

Emboldened by this success, one evening they launched Mr. Pingo to the moon. The staff had built a fake moon out of papier-mâché, and the plan was to blast Mr. Pingo off the earth and then lower him down to the fake moon surface in a capsule. As usual, the studio was filled with people that night, everyone getting ready for the next program. A choir from a local church had come in and were all squeezed over to one side in their choir robes, waiting for Mr. Pingo to finish so they could get on the set for the next half hour.

But when Mr. Pingo was launched off the earth, too much stage powder was used. It was pretty realistic and filled the entire studio with blinding, choking smoke. Since the choir was downwind from Mr. Pingo, they got the worst of it. Everyone was coughing, choking, and gagging, and Cousin Neil had to shout at Mr. Pingo to make him hear. "They told us there weren't any people up here on the moon, but I can hear them out there in the darkness, can't you?"

And Mr. Pingo squeaked back, "I sure can."

One thing was sure, we certainly impressed the kids who were watching that night.

The thing that amazed me most was that people were watching. Calls were pouring into the station from all over Tidewater. We had to get a larger mailbox to handle the volume of mail. With the mail (Praise the Lord), we started getting some contributions, since we were making it plain that we were not going to accept advertising to keep this Christian station on the air.

And we were on the air. We started out broadcasting from seven until ten every night. Three hours a day was all we could manage with our limited staff and equipment. Later we expanded that to four hours, 6:00 P.M. until 10:00 P.M. Finally we moved from 5:00 P.M.

until midnight. We never dreamed at that time that we might one day be broadcasting on a network of radio stations twenty-four hours a day.

One of our biggest needs was program material. Live television is a terrible strain, since you must always have something before the camera. We had only a few free travelog films that we used to round out the day or fill in blank spots.

Neil had been raised in an Assembly of God church and never had been exposed to worldly amusements. As a result, he wasn't able to effectively screen the films we used. One night we put on a film showing a jet airliner on an overseas flight. The pleasures of the trip were being highlighted by the airline company, and they were climaxed by the serving of some sort of beverage by the stewardess. I was in the control room, half-watching the monitor, when I noticed something. "Neil, they're pouring Manhattans! We're serving liquor over our Christian station!"

Neil kept looking at the film and said, "No, Pat, that's coffee. See —the stewardess has it in that funny little container, and she's shaking it up to mix the coffee and sugar."

"That's not coffee!" I shouted. "You've never seen a cocktail shaker in action. I've lived around those things for *years*! I've *used* them! That's a Manhattan she's serving!"

By the time we got through arguing, the film was over, and the scene had been broadcast over the Lord's station. I was afraid to answer the telephone the rest of the evening, knowing some irate financial supporter would call and say that if this was the kind of junk we were going to broadcast, he'd withhold his three dollars and send it someplace else.

We simply weren't able to screen all the films we used, and they were a constant source of embarrassment. Every once in a while I would stand unbelieving in front of the monitor while some Polynesian hootchy-cootchy dancer wiggled her way across the screen, or some dignified man held up a bottle of beer and recommended it for all the viewers out there in TV-land. All I could do was pray the

Lord would provide us with a better class of films and programs, and in the meantime so arrange the atmospheric conditions that the transmission of these particular portions of the film would be disrupted.

We just didn't have enough material. We used everything the denominations had to offer: Southern Baptists, Lutherans, and Episcopals. We used Billy Graham, Oral Roberts, and Kathryn Kuhlman—but these were all just half-hour shows, and they didn't begin to use up the time we needed to fill the evening. I was on the air much of the time. I taught the International Sunday School Lesson every Saturday night on a program called "Tomorrow's Lesson." I also had a program called "Teach In" where viewers phoned in their questions and I tried to answer them. We were innovating, and had borrowed a 35 mm lens for the camera which, although it distorted the depth perception, made our tiny studio look twice as big. However, I soon learned—from the rash of phone calls—that every time I gestured and pointed at the camera, my finger looked like a telephone pole.

Besides John Stallings, we were also drawing on other local talent. One of the viewers' favorites was a tiny, ancient woman named Emma McSmith. Mrs. McSmith had been a newspaper reporter at the Scopes trial and had been teaching the Bible for more than sixty years. Although in her eighties, she was still a dynamic teacher, with as much poise on camera as any professional entertainer.

One Sunday afternoon she arrived at the station late. It was almost time for her to go on the air. It had been snowing, and the parking lot was dark. Rushing in through the doorway, she stepped in a deep puddle, which filled her shoes with icy water. Undaunted, she walked into the studio and stood before the camera for thirty minutes, teaching the Bible and reminding the viewers of God's love—all with her shoes filled with ice water. Despite her age, Emma McSmith never missed a Sunday teaching.

I knew that our makeshift efforts were a beginning, however inept they seemed. My heart longed for an audience big enough to justify really outstanding programs. I looked at the map of the east coast—

at least 40 million people lived between Norfolk and Boston. There had to be a Christian network of television stations for the east coast.

Then I thumbtacked on the wall of my office a big map of the United States. Rough circles had been penciled around Los Angeles, Atlanta, Philadelphia, Indianapolis, and Norfolk. These cities seemed to be key geographic spots which could serve as major production centers for Christian television programs. From each city, programs by tape, or line, or microwave could be fed to secular or religious stations all over the country.

Before I left New York, Paul Morris and I had laid a big map of the United States on the table in his study. We carefully marked the appropriate cities and marched around the table with our hands raised to God, claiming them for him.

Our original charter included the vision of just such a network, although at the time we had no idea how it was going to come about. In fact, after we began broadcasting, our major problem was getting our 17,000 watts to the city limits. In those days, just reaching across the Hampton Roads Harbor to Newport News was a major achievement.

XVII

What Do You Think about
When You Shave?

———
———
———

Our biggest problem was money—or rather the lack of it. We had started with no capital and were determined not to solicit funds on the air. Nor did we allow any commercial advertising, although on several occasions we were strongly tempted. As long as we didn't overextend ourselves and go too far in debt, I felt we could manage, although our total operating expenses for the first month were only $460. Yet even with me drawing no salary, and the station staff getting paid only if there was enough money left over, we were still just hours away from financial disaster.

"Dede," I said one Sunday afternoon after we had come home from church, "Norfolk is full of wealthy men who, I think, would be delighted to help in this ministry if they just knew about it."

"Go on," Dede said, looking at me over the top of her glasses as she sat on the sofa mending a torn pair of trousers.

"Well, I was just thinking. What we need is an advisory board—wealthy men, professional men, who will meet with us and help us with our problems."

"What problems?" Dede said, pulling off her glasses and looking up at me.

"Well, we need some sound financial advice," I said.

"You think these men could help tell you how to spend what you don't have, is that it?"

I knew what Dede was driving at, but I was just bullheaded enough to stick with my proposition. "It wouldn't hurt to let them know that we don't have any money," I said. "I wouldn't ask them for anything, just give them the information, and they could do what the Lord told them to do."

"The Lord has already told you to do something—that's to trust in him and walk by faith. Now you're trying to manipulate people to do what God has promised he'd do for you. I don't like it."

I should have listened to her, but instead, I made a select list of respected business and professional men in the city and called them together for a breakfast meeting at the Golden Triangle, a brand-new hotel in the heart of the city.

We met in a plush dining room on the mezzanine, and after a big breakfast I outlined our needs and plans. The men seemed excited enough, and there was a great deal of discussion, with a lot of "Mr. Chairman," "I propose," "I amend the proposal," and the like. When it was over, they all left, and I was stuck with the bill for the breakfast.

I had one more meeting with this same group over at the station. Again we made the mistake of serving a meal, and again the station had to pick up the tab. I was learning how these men had made their fortunes—or at least how they kept them. I decided to let the advisory council die. It wasn't accomplishing anything and was costing us more money than we could afford.

Yet every day we were faced with the possibility of economic annihilation. If God were to withdraw his hand for a single day, we'd go under. We had no reserves and were under constant pressure just to pay for the tubes and pieces of lumber needed to build props. It was becoming an unbearable situation.

Invitations were coming in from various chapters of the Full Gospel Business Men, and I accepted as many as I could. This gave me an opportunity to share my vision of a worldwide network ministry. This, however, combined with the staggering pace I was keeping at the church and the station, kept me constantly on the verge of exhaustion. One Saturday night as I sat on camera teaching "Tomorrow's Lesson," I was so groggy that my eyes slowly closed as I taught. Before I knew it, I was asleep. I continued talking, and my spirit, realizing what had happened, jerked me back to consciousness. At other times I knew I appeared so tired that the viewers thought I was drugged.

Then one day, in one of our staff prayer meetings, several of the local supporters had come in. One of them was Mercedes Morales, an active Baptist laywoman who had been filled with the Holy Spirit. I had just returned from another jaunt and was sitting half-asleep when she began to prophesy. The message hit me in the stomach like an ironclad fist, jerking me into full consciousness: "You go to the north and to the south and to the east and to the west to seek all manner of grand things, when I have given you a field that is white unto harvest. I want you to reap that harvest. You have ignored the field I have given you."

I sat in my chair too stunned to speak. This was God's message for me. I had been thinking in terms of Indianapolis, Philadelphia, Atlanta, and Los Angeles, when God wanted me to think about Tidewater. I was proclaiming the need for a network when God wanted me to work at the needs of WYAH-TV.

That Thursday night, after we put the station to bed, and I was driving home, I realized that although God had given me the vision of a network, I was going astray by looking for early fulfillment when it wasn't God's time.

"It sure looks like you're missing out on some tremendous opportunities, God," I said as I pulled up in front of the house, "but I guess you know what you're doing."

That night I promised God I would spend every Friday, beginning the next day, from dawn until after noon in prayer and fasting. The very next morning God spoke to me while I was praying and waiting before him. "Congress is going to pass a bill requiring all television sets to be equipped with UHF."

I could hardly believe that this was from God. The bill had come up several times in Congress already, and each time it had been laughed back into committee where it had died. Besides, I thought such a bill was unconstitutional, and therefore I never shared, specifically, what God told me.

It was two years later when I got a phone call from my father on Capitol Hill. "Son, the UHF bill has been brought up again, and President Kennedy has given it his backing. I believe it's going to be passed into law."

I got busy, pleading with Christian groups to purchase the existing UHF stations which could be picked up for a song. But no one would listen. There was no vision. Then the bill was passed and signed into law, requiring all television sets manufactured after April 1964 to be equipped with UHF as well as VHF receivers. Several Christians finally got together and tried to buy up some of the UHF stations, but by then they were so expensive that only the large commercial firms could afford to purchase them.

Harald Bredesen, commenting on the matter, said, "How come God didn't know about all those good deals?"

"He did," I said, "but no one would listen to him."

Yet even with this, I could see God's hand in guidance. In those early days we had no real concept of how to minister on television. Had we obtained more than one TV station in those days, we never would have developed God's plan for spiritual television, because we would have been too busy getting our stations on the air. It's as though God always intends for his people to start small and build, for it takes time and struggle to learn what God really wants us to do.

During the spring of 1962, I called Stewart Brinsfield in Baltimore. "Brother, when do you want to take over operation of this radio station you bought? We never have drawn up the sale document."

"I've been meaning to call you for several weeks, Pat," he said. "God won't let me have that station. You'll have to take it back."

"But what about the $5,000? I can't pay it back."

"Just give me a note," he said, "and pay it back when you can."

Thus, without notice, we were again owners of an FM radio station.

Warren Brenning, a friend of Harald's from Oregon, wrote me that he was interested in coming to work for us in the radio station. We told him that we were strained financially and might not have enough money to pay his salary. Besides, we were not going to take money out of the TV ministry to subsidize the radio station. However, if he wanted to come, we'd make him program director for the radio station and trust God to supply the funds.

Brenning arrived—with six children. I could see where we were going to have to trust God a lot more than we imagined at first.

But before we could begin putting the radio station into shape, we had to have the electrical power turned on, and the power company demanded a $200 deposit first. They might as well have demanded $2,000. I told Warren to get his family settled, and we'd go to work to pray that God would provide the funds.

The next Sunday morning I preached at the Park View Baptist Church in Portsmouth. Later that day, before the evening service, I was in the study when there was a soft knock at the door. One of the members came in and said timidly, "This morning, while you were preaching, God spoke to me and told me to give $100 to his work. I don't know where to give it and thought maybe you would know someplace where it could be used." With that he handed me a check for $100 and walked out.

"Praise the Lord!" I shouted as soon as the door closed. The next morning I was standing at the door of the power company when it opened. "I can't give you $200," I told the clerk, "but here's $100."

"Just a minute," she said and disappeared into the back room.

Moments later she was out, shaking her head in amazement. "They've really been cracking down on these deposits with so many people running off without paying their bill . . ." Her voice faded off. "But this morning the boss didn't even look at your application. He just said, 'It'll be all right.' You'll have your power on by three o'clock this afternoon."

It was another miraculous intervention. I knew now that God intended for us to get into the radio ministry as well as TV.

The station had been located in a garage and had a homemade antenna on top of a seventy-foot creosoted pole. When the wind blew, the elements would shake and arc, and electric sparks would fly all over the place. the first time we turned on the transmitter, the transmission lines burned out in three sections because the antenna didn't match up as it should. We later learned that the transmitter was the first FM transmitter manufactured. It was so old and creaky that Warren used to lay hands on it and pray, asking the Holy Spirit to heal it of its diseases and restore it to original power.

We changed the call letters to WXRI-FM (XRI being the first three letters in the Greek word for Christ—the Anointed One), and on August 3, Harald Bredesen came down and stood with Dede and me in our living room as we turned the radio on at 7:00 A.M. and heard the station sign on the air with the "Hallelujah Chorus." We lifted our hands and in awe praised God that we could be part of his eternal purpose.

Radio programming is much easier than TV programming, for there is an abundance of excellent Christian record albums, most of which can be obtained free of charge. Our format was all Christian, and as on TV we accepted no commercial advertising. We ran old standard programs such as the "Old-Fashioned Revival Hour," "Billy Graham," and "Back to the Bible." For music there was Bev Shea, Tony Fontaine, Alan McGill, The Haven of Rest Quartette, and many others. And the people loved it.

In fact, they loved it so much that within three months WXRI-FM had nosed out nearly all the other AM and FM stations in Tidewater and was ranked number five in popularity among the more than twenty radio stations in the area. Among those we passed in popularity were the 5,000-watt NBC station in Portsmouth and the 5,000-watt ABC station in Newport News.

But it was hard work. I was on the air as much as twelve hours a day some days as Warren and I exchanged shifts. We were able to train several high school students who volunteered and finally hired one woman on a part-time basis to handle all traffic and secretarial work for the station. Even though our income increased very little, our ministry increased a hundredfold.

It was this success factor that finally got me in trouble with my church. I knew it was coming, because I was giving a great deal of time to the communications ministry. In January the chairman of the special committee from the deacons came into my office at the church. "Pat, the committee has met and decided we need you full time at the church or you'll have to leave."

"But I am putting in between forty and fifty hours a week. By any standard that's full time for a $100-a-week job."

"Yes, we realize that," he said, "but what do you think about when you shave in the morning?"

I didn't have the heart to tell him that one of the things I thought about was getting him saved, for even though he was chairman of the special committee, he never had been born again. However, I knew what he was talking about. They wanted a Minister of Education who ate, slept, and breathed his job—and I wasn't doing that. I was working at it, and we were having a good measure of success, but my heart was in the television and radio ministry.

"You'll have to make a decision," he said. "Either the church gets your full attention and you give up the television ministry, or you resign your job and let us get someone who will do what we expect of them."

"I'm sorry," I said. "You leave me no choice. God has given me this ministry of television, and even though in my own mind I am unable to separate it from the ministry of the church, if I am forced to make a choice, I must choose the television."

That afternoon I sat down and wrote out my resignation. I had no idea where our personal support was going to come from, but again I committed the entire matter to God and promised him I would wait for him to provide.

I didn't have to wait long. Two days after I left the church I was visited at the television station by two men I had never seen before. "We're on the pulpit committee at the Parkview Baptist Church here in Portsmouth," they said. "We need a supply pastor for several months while we're searching for a permanent minister. We understand you might be available."

I knew the church well. It was a 1,100-member church located just a few blocks from the TV station.

"I'd love to do it, but this television ministry is consuming my full time."

"We understand that and don't want you to take a moment away from it. All we want you to do is preach two sermons on Sunday, hold a Bible study on Wednesday night, marry the wed, and bury the dead. Nothing else."

For this they offered me $100 a week and at the same time I would be spending only half a day on the job, have less responsibility, and be my own boss. Once again God had shut a good door in order to open a far better one.

My service to Parkview Church lasted six months. During this time I often had to take money from my own salary to help pay the bills at the station or to share with those who were working and drawing little or no money. At the end of the six months, my ministry terminated, the church having called a full-time pastor. Again I was without salary and having to trust God totally to supply our needs.

One of the last things I did before leaving Parkview Church was to get permission to use their mailing list to send out a letter asking the people to give their prayer support to the television ministry. I believed that if people everywhere began praying, God would supply all our needs, and I wanted to enlist as many prayer partners as possible.

On Friday, before my last service on Sunday, I drove out to see Mr. Fred Beasley, a local philanthropist who had been instrumental in starting Frederick College in Portsmouth. I understood the college might be interested in using some of the services of our television station for educational TV programs and wanted to discuss the matter with him. But God had another purpose in mind.

Mr. Beasley was a multimillionaire who had made his fortune in the ice and coal business across the south. He had given millions of dollars away, mostly to colleges and prep schools.

When I was ushered into his office, he gave me a strange look and said, "This is odd. I've been looking for you, and now you have walked in here. It *must* be God's will that we get together."

I was puzzled and asked, "What do you mean, Mr. Beasley? You don't even know why I've come to see you."

"That makes little difference," he said, getting up from his desk and walking around to where I was sitting. "You probably don't even know it, but I'm on the mailing list of the Parkview Baptist Church, and when I got your letter the other day, I knew God was telling me that I should help you out."

"You mean the station?" I said hopefully.

"No, I don't mean the station. I mean you, personally."

"What do you want to do?" I said, never having been on the receiving end of a situation like this.

"I want to supply you with a salary; then you won't have to take any of the contributions for yourself, and you can give all your time and energy to the station."

I gulped and tried to say something, but my words never got past the top of my throat.

"Well, how much do you need to live on?"

Again I tried to say something, but nothing came out. How do you answer a question like that?

"I'll tell you what to do," Mr. Beasley said, sensing that I was having some difficulty arriving at an answer, or even arriving at a vocabulary for that matter. "You come back Monday and tell me."

Monday morning I was back in his office. "God has told me to tell you I need $100 a week."

"One hundred dollars a week?" he said, crinkling his brow. "Are you sure that is enough?"

"If it was for the station, I would ask for ten times as much," I said. "But since you made it plain that it was for me, then God said to give you that figure. That's the figure we've lived on for almost two years, and we can continue to live on it now."

"How would you like it?" he asked. "I can give it to you personally from me to you, or I can give it to you from my foundation to you. Either way, it makes no difference to me."

"I think it would be better if you'd give it to me personally. This way I am not involved with the board of directors at your foundation, nor will I have the feeling that I am working for your foundation."

"Good thinking," he said. "Anytime you don't need it, you tell me, and anytime I don't want to give it to you, I'll tell you. We'll just keep it simple, and every month I'll have my secretary mail you a check for $433.33, which is $100.00 a week prorated out over thirteen weeks in a quarter. You can pick up your first check when you leave this morning."

I could hardly believe what God was doing. I had drawn my last check at the church the night before, and this morning I was back on the payroll of God's Kingdom.

"Now since I don't think that $100 a week is a living wage," he continued, "I want to give you something else. God has blessed my wife and me with a fortune, and we intend to see it all goes back into some phase of his work. We have a nice little house right near your TV station, and we'd like for you to have it, rent free, as long as you like. It's been empty for some time, and we want it occupied. What do you say?"

I said yes.

But after I saw the house, I wished I had said something else.

"I refuse to live here," Dede said as we walked through the old slum house located three blocks south of the station in a fast-deteriorating area. "I don't care if it is free; we ought to be able to live where we want to live."

The two-story house had been newly painted, but had never been in good condition. There were cracks in the floor—in some places at least a quarter of an inch separating the boards—and since there was no subflooring, the damp, cold winter wind swept up through the floor, causing the curtains on the windows to wave in the draft.

"Well, we'll just have to yield ourselves to the Lord," I said.

"But I can't stand it," Dede said with a determined look on her face. "Nor can I yield myself to the Lord when we're thrust into a slum house that has only one closet upstairs and one closet down-stairs and is in the middle of a neighborhood where our children are liable to pick up every disease in the world."

While we were talking, Mr. Beasley's nephew walked in. He was all smiles. "I hadn't seen this old place since we got it painted, but it looks great, doesn't it?"

Dede scowled at him, and I tried to cover up. "We can't begin to tell you how much we appreciate your uncle's generosity."

"The nice part about it is it's only a few blocks from the station," he said. "Most ministers wouldn't be satisfied to live in a place like this, but you're different. That's the reason my uncle wants you to have it."

I sensed Dede was about to explode, and thanking Mr. Beasley's nephew again, I hustled her out to the car. "I'll not live there," she said. "I'll not bring my children up in an environment like this."

But she did. We moved in the next week and lived there two years. One thing about the old house: it was bad, but it was great compared to the neighborhood. Living next door to us was a blonde woman whose Oriental husband was at sea with the navy. She had five children, and her husband's cousin had moved in with her to keep her company. They had some of the wildest parties imaginable —right under our bedroom window. Dede had the cultural experience of hearing for the first time words she didn't even know existed.

Across the street was a fifteen-year-old juvenile delinquent who had dropped out of school. She would come out and stand under the streetlight in the middle of the night and scream filthy oaths up and down the street. Behind our house was a graveyard. In the winter we froze, and in the summer we suffocated. Some things, I found out, are almost intolerable even if they are free.

After two years of this, I determined that to keep my sanity and my marriage together I was going to have to do something. I asked a friend of mine to draw up a scale model of an old homestead which had once belonged to one of my distant relatives. It was a perfect example of Georgian architecture, and I just drooled, thinking how nice it would be to live in a house where the children could have room to move around and I could have a horse or two in the back.

I went to see Mr. Beasley, thinking he might give me some land to build on. "What would you think of the idea of me building a house out in the country?" I asked.

He looked at me coldly and said, "I think it's a lousy idea. Why should you build a house when I have an empty house out in the country you could live in? I don't want to hurt you with kindness, but if you're not satisfied with where you are, you can move into this other house."

I caught my breath and said, "I'll go home and ask the Lord if I should move or not."

"Well, if the Lord tells you to build a house, he's wrong," Beasley said.

"Absolutely not!" Dede cried when I told her of Mr. Beasley's offer to let us move into another one of his vacant houses. "Don't think I'm not grateful for his generosity. But it's time we have a house of our own."

"The least we can do is go out and look at it," I said. "He says it's in the country and has lots of room and has been boarded up for five years."

"I knew it," Dede said sarcastically. "Anytime you find a house that is so bad nobody will live in it for five years, you've found a house that is so bad that nobody will live in it."

"Well, I'm going out to see it. If you want to come along, you can."

A woman's curiosity is her weakest point, and moments later Dede was in the car beside me as we drove west out of Portsmouth, across the river, and into the country.

"The house is supposed to be located on the back side of the property that belongs to Frederick College," I said, turning in the old driveway at the entrance to the college. The concrete road wound through a heavily wooded section and then opened into a large pasture. At the far side of the pasture, we could see the house. We caught our breath. It was magnificent.

It was an old southern mansion with four white columns across the front, surrounded by huge magnolia trees. There was a large barn nearby. The house had four bedrooms with baths upstairs and down. There was a formal living room and formal dining room, a den, a spacious kitchen, and space—open space everywhere.

All my life I had wanted a place where I could raise horses and play the role of a gentleman farmer, and now here it was, handed to me free. The college would supply us water, mow our grass, pick up our garbage, and give us access to all the acres we wanted to use as our own.

That night, after we got back to our slum house, I prayed, "Lord, you know how badly I want that house. But I will not move unless you tell me to move. I've made too many mistakes going against your will, and since I don't have the funds to move, you'll have to provide them as a sign if you want me out there."

I opened my Bible and began reading from Genesis 22. It was the story of Abraham taking his son Isaac to the mountain to offer him as a sacrifice. God had provided the ram in the thicket, and then I read, "And Abraham called the name of that place Jehovah-jireh; as it is said to this day, In the mount of the lord it shall be provided."

I ran up the stairs, causing the entire house to shake as my feet pounded against the bare boards. "Praise the Lord! Listen to this, Dede: God has said he will provide—this day."

And God did. The following morning a friend offered to help move us. Another friend called and offered to do some painting, and another volunteered to help with the carpentry work to fix up the place. By the middle of September we had moved—into the biggest and finest house I'd ever dreamed of living in.

That first evening, after all our friends had left, Dede and I carried two chairs out under the huge Civil War magnolia tree in the front yard. Sitting there in the cool of twilight, watching the last haze of Indian summer fade from the sky, Dede reached over and took my hand. "Forgive me for my impatience," she said.

Then with a tear trickling down her face she looked upward and said, "From now on, Lord, I shall try to remember what you said— 'Be patient and complain not, God will provide.' "

XVIII

Sharing and Believing

Tremendous pressure was being put on me from the staff to accept commercial advertisements. Most of our original staff had moved on and we had a new crew coming to work for us. These men and women didn't understand the original concepts God had given us and felt strongly we were passing up a great source of income by denying ourselves commercial advertising. "We just can't make it without additional funds," several said heatedly.

Things were tough, and the financial strain had almost doubled since we opened the radio station. Our monthly income from contributions was increasing slowly, but not nearly enough to keep up with the needs. It was a killing proposition.

In my Friday morning prayer time I went before the Lord with several alternate plans. One was to get out of the business, but I got an immediate negative answer from God on that. Another was to sell commercials. Again I received a check from God. A third plan had to do with daily financial reports, which we would give out over the air. However, to me, this was simply begging in disguise, which is worse than straight begging, and was like the plan I had when I called the advisory board together.

Finally I came to the concept of faith partners. Each month Dede and I, along with the staff, were forced to trust God for the money to operate the stations. It was time to ask the listeners and viewers to add their faith to ours. If our monthly budget was $7,000, we had to trust God to supply all of it. Now we would ask 700 people to trust God for $10 each—not necessarily from what they had, but from what he would send them. Each year we would have a telethon for the expenses of the coming year. This would not just be a telethon to raise money; it would be a roll call of faith.

In the fall of 1963 we had our first telethon. We went on the air telling our audience about our needs for the following year and asking them to believe with us that God would raise the $7,000 needed for each month's budget. I asked our viewers to believe with me that God would raise up 700 people who would trust him to supply $10 apiece each month for the coming year. We called the telethon, "The 700 Club," and as the people called in, we recorded their pledges.

We put several telephones in the studio and invited guests in to sing and share while the telephoned pledges were being recorded. By the end of the weekend we had monthly pledges of $3,500, which was only half of what we had asked for, but far more than we had ever received before. I knew this was God's plan for meeting our financial needs.

It was at this time that I became aware of a tremendous attack of Satan against our work. I tried to praise God for it, because I knew that Satan's attacks come when we are on the verge of a spiritual breakthrough; but this one was so strong and so powerful that I was almost swept away myself. Without warning, Satan began diverting our attention and dividing us internally. I found myself in one of the most horrible, tension-filled episodes of my life.

Harald Bredesen had recommended a young lady from Ohio to come as our program director. She was a commercial copywriter, and a good one. But as a program director she was in over her head. Not only that, she was not spiritually mature enough to roll with the punches that were getting thrown at us in this faith venture. Almost as soon as she was on the job, she began to criticize and ridicule our procedures. I knew our methods were not orthodox, but since no one had ever gone before us to show us how to operate a Spirit-directed

TV station, we had to feel our way along. We were determined we would not be hamstrung by too many scripts or time schedules, and if the Holy Spirit was moving while someone was talking or singing on camera, we were not going to cut him off just because the hour changed on the clock.

Our new program director couldn't dream of running a TV station like that, and she set out to try to change things. Her method was to cut me down behind my back to other station personnel, all of whom were under financial and spiritual pressure. It didn't take long before staff relations were seething as some people took sides, others quit, and still others were actively at work trying to destroy the station's concept of ministry.

By the end of the year, the entire staff was boiling in discontent. A full-scale mutiny was waiting to happen. It was during this time that I was desperately trying to convince other Christians to buy up UHF stations in major cities before passage of the UHF bill ran their value out of sight. Yet we didn't have enough money to pay our own bills, and the Christian Broadcasting Network was about to come apart at the seams.

When you're in the midst of a battle, it's difficult to sit back and philosophize. I guess that my inner spirit witnessed that this was Satan's trick to try to destroy us, but I was so busy fighting a defensive battle that I didn't have time to sit down and look at his overall battle plan. Had I been able, I would have seen that Satan was trying to destroy us by infiltrating our organization with all sorts of strange people. I was so desperate for help that I indiscriminately took anybody who came along with a Christian testimony. I was always apologetic because I couldn't pay more money, and as a result everybody who worked for us thought they were doing us a favor. Most of our volunteers were immature and caused more problems than they were solving. I made the additional mistake of treating them as though they all had the same spiritual maturity as I did, when actually very few of them knew anything about the ways of God's Spirit. They didn't understand the struggle we were in; they didn't understand why we weren't a commercial station; they didn't understand the Holy Spirit's method of programming; and everyone was in turmoil.

Even more frightening was the fact that this same spirit seemed to descend over all Tidewater. The Edgar Cayce Foundation was making a big play for the minds of people. Hugh Cayce, Edgar's son, was the Sunday-school superintendent at the First Presbyterian Church in Virginia Beach. There was a terrific appeal for denominational people to believe in reincarnation, and there were springing up many small "prayer" groups that believed in this Satanic doctrine. The Spiritualist Church was making a resurgence. People were calling in from all over Tidewater pleading with us to pray because their loved ones were being caught up in seances and occult groups. The whole area was rife with Satan's power.

Dennis Bennett, the Episcopal priest who had been one of the leaders in the charismatic movement, visited in the area. "What is it that I sense here?" he said, after spending two days with us. "I feel some strange presence of oppression that I have never felt before."

We explained the terrible binding and blinding power of spiritualism. Before he left that weekend, Bennett got a full dose of Satanic oppression.

Kenneth Hagin, Spirit-led Bible teacher from Texas, visited us. He said he had never seen such a Satanic onslaught against a Christian ministry. Satan had used the same kind of onslaught, Hagin told us, to try to destroy Jesus when he was a baby.

"The only way to combat this thing is through prayer," he said. "There is a desperate need to get some kind of prayer ministry started so that all the people in Tidewater can join hands in prayer and punch through the umbrella of Satanic oppression covering this place. You need reinforcement from God. You're in a battle to the death, brother, and prayer is the only thing that is going to win it for you."

One Friday morning as I was praying, God revealed to me that there was such a thing as a spirit of poverty. "This spirit," he revealed, "can fasten itself on my men and my work like a tick on a dog until it sucks all the life out of it. It is the spirit, plus the spirit of dissension, which is suffocating my work in Tidewater."

"But Lord," I anguished back in prayer, "how can we be delivered from such a spirit? I've invoked the name of Jesus, and the blood of Jesus, and I've fasted and prayed, and it is still here."

"Let all the people pray," God said. "Let all the people pray."

We had the means of calling the people together in prayer through television, but our transmitter was so weak that the signal barely carried across the bay. I did know that a climate of faith was being built up among our regular listeners, despite the horrible dissension at the station. Besides that, we were daily receiving reports of people who were coming to Christ, even being healed. I knew that there were groups of Spirit-filled people in Newport News and Hampton, godly people who would join us in prayer, but we needed more power—spiritually and from the transmitter.

A new FM radio transmitter would cost $11,000, and that was the cheapest on the market. Yet as I was praying before God the next week, he said to me, "Pat, I want you to have an RCA transmitter."

I sat straight up. "Lord, we can't even raise $11,000! The RCA transmitter is the most expensive on the market! Where will we get the $19,000 to buy one?"

"Wait on me, be faithful to your calling, and I will provide," the familiar voice in my heart said.

Yet no money came to buy any kind of transmitter, not even enough for a down payment. And the old transmitter was about to die. Every day when we cut it on, there was an unspoken prayer that it would last through the day.

The new year came and dropped behind and still no money. Then, the first of March, 1964, I received word that RCA was going to unwrap a brand-new line of transmitters. They had been using a particular style for more than ten years. Now there had been a tremendous scientific breakthrough, and RCA had developed a new type transmitter which was years ahead of all the others on the market. Now I knew why God had held back the down-payment money. He did not want us to use his money to buy out-of-date equipment.

I went on the air telling our audience that we had set the month of March as a month to believe God that the down payment of $10,000 would be supplied. We were going to claim an entire new installation—new transmitter, new antenna, new everything—and trust God to give us the money before the month was over.

Again Satan worked among the members of our staff. "We don't need a larger transmitter," one staff member said on the air one night. "All we need to do is trust God to perform a miracle on this old one. If God wants the message to get out, he'll perform a miracle to see it gets out." This kind of talk was almost mutiny, but I was so tied up in details that all I could do was moan about it and plead with God to do "something."

That "something" God did was to turn me back to his Word. The first Friday morning in March, I was fasting and praying, and halfway through the morning, the Holy Spirit prompted me to discontinue my fast and eat a late breakfast. As I was sitting at the kitchen table, I flipped open my Bible, and a verse seemed to leap at me from the page: "They that are far off shall come and build in the temple of the Lord" (Zech. 6:15). I knew at once what was going to happen. I knew we were going to get the money, and it was going to come from distant places.

The next day a special-delivery letter arrived at our front door. It was from a woman in Long Island, writing, "I feel guided to send you this check." I unfolded the check and looked at it. It was for $3,000.

A week later an old friend from North Carolina wrote and said, "Praise God. I've had $1,000 in my tithe account and didn't know what to do with it. The Holy Spirit has told me to send it to you."

Then, on March 31, I was awakened about midnight by a call from an old friend, Larry Hammond, in Texas. Larry knew of our situation and had taken it on himself to try to raise a little money to help us buy the transmitter. "Pat, I'm calling from Texas, and I have $1,000 for you."

"Praise the Lord!" I shouted over the phone, throwing back the covers. "It's coming from as far away as Texas. That's half of what we need."

"I've got something else," he said. "This same man who is giving the $1,000 says he will co-sign a note for whatever you need to finish the project."

"Does he have the kind of money we need to back it?" I asked.

"I think so," Larry stammered. "Anyway, he said he'd be glad to go on the note with you."

"This is fantastic! You mean to tell me that a man I've never met and who knows absolutely nothing about our ministry will go on a note with me? Who is he?"

"He is a vice-president of Furr's, Inc., in Lubbock."

"Hallelujah! Thank you, Jesus!" I shouted, waking the entire household. "It's March 31, and the money has come from far off, just like the Lord promised."

The next morning I made a quick trip to our bank telling the banker that we had figured up all our needs, including the price of installation of the new transmitter and FM antenna, and would need to borrow $10,000 on a note endorsed by my unknown friend from Texas. The banker was less than enthusiastic but said, "We'll check out this benefactor in Lubbock and let you know."

A week later I got a call from the loan officer in the bank. "Mr. Robertson, we've heard from your friend in Texas."

From the tone of his voice, I felt my heart sinking. Suddenly I was fearful it was going to be just another one of those straws you grasp which promises much but delivers nothing. "Well, what's the story?"

"He sent us a balance sheet, and you can have anything you want."

"What do you mean," I stammered, "anything I want?"

"I mean your Texan is a millionaire. Whatever amount you want, you can come down and pick up."

"Praise the Lord," I said. "Make me out a check for $10,000 and I'll be down in half an hour to pick it up."

I never met our friend in Texas. I never talked to him and have not heard from him since. I simply look upon this as another of God's amazing miracles.

When the transmitter was delivered, the third one to be installed by RCA, it gave us the most powerful FM signal in the area. God really knew what he was talking about when he told me not to go second class, but to wait on him. Now, at last, we were equipped for battle.

XIX

There's Something in the Air

———
———
———

Thanksgiving Day, 1963, found me nailing roof rafters on our new building. The building was designed to hold the new transmitter we planned to buy, as well as our expanded radio facilities. "You've got too much space here," one of my friends said as he helped me hoist two-by-sixes overhead. "Twenty-five by fifty-five is far more room than you'll ever need." Little did we know.

However, some things were obvious at the time. At 50,000 watts, WXRI was now the most powerful radio station in Tidewater. We were broadcasting twenty-four hours a day from our 300-foot tower, and overnight our audience quadrupled. The radio station, which in 1962 had almost sent us into bankruptcy, had by the fall of 1964 become *the* station in Tidewater.

The day we went on the air with our new transmitter, in fact, the moment we shifted the signal from the old station to the new one, the old FM transmitter gasped and died. We later tried to revive it, but it was simply worn out. It wasn't difficult to see God's timing in the entire matter.

Overnight we made contact with all the prayer groups and praying Christians in the Tidewater area. Within days we began to receive letters and phone calls from all over the area as people contacted us to thank us for the blessing of touching their homes and lives with the message of Christ. Instantly we sensed a rollback of the Satanic oppression that had blanketed our ministry for the last two years.

Suddenly we were on the winning side, rather than the losing end.

In 1965 Jay Arlan joined our staff. Jay had been program director for Billy Graham's radio stations WFGW and WMIT-FM in Black Mountain, North Carolina. Prior to that he had been ABC's top announcer, having handled programs like their Breakfast Club and Paul Harvey News. Jay brought to CBN the professionalism I had so long prayed for.

Even more significant than his arrival was the answer to my prayer that God supply us with someone to minister to children. Neil Eskelin had left, and a succession of amateurs had tried their hand at a children's show, but all had failed miserably. I knew that a ministry to children was the key to Christian television, for it was children who soak up forty or more hours of television each week.

Jim and Tammy Bakker were traveling Assembly of God evangelists, but prior to his conversion Jim had been a rock-'n'-roll disc jockey for teenage dances. The thing that attracted me to them was their ability with children. Both were extremely young (Jim was twenty-five and Tammy was twenty-three) and good looking. Tammy, only 4'10" tall, looked like a kid herself, and they had developed a puppet routine which drew kids to their meetings in droves.

They first went on the air in September 1965 with a program called "Come on Over." Jim had an easy-does-it way before the camera, but Tammy, who had never been on the air before, took one look at the naked eye of the camera with its blinking red signal light and went speechless. The cameraman, sensing her fright, shifted the focus to Jim, and the audience never suspected what was happening. Tammy soon overcame her fright, and the two of them began to make a terrific impact on our viewers—especially the kids. They were young and alive and full of ideas, and when Jim made the announcement over the air that they wanted to have a big Halloween party at the studio for the children of the area, we were literally swamped with kids who swarmed into the station. From that moment on, we knew something was happening through the ministry of Jim and Tammy Bakker.

Quality television programming costs money, and our bills were mounting up in staggering proportions. By the end of the summer in 1965 we were $40,000 in debt.

Yet, for the first time, I felt that we had the personnel to make the station go. We had added to our staff Bill Gregory, a topflight television engineer from the local NBC outlet; Bill Garthwaite, who had years of experience in television production; and Joyce Radford, a vivacious but deeply spiritual young lady who served as combination office manager, bookkeeper, and secretary. John Carraway, a Baptist minister, who had been the MC of a very popular gospel music program on a local radio station, had also felt led to join us. In my judgment these people combined with Jay Arlan and Jim and Tammy made a good team.

Feeling that they were with me, I summoned the courage to go to Mr. Beasley to ask for a loan of $40,000 to cover our needs. I started out by asking advice.

"Looks to me from your books," Mr. Beasley said, "that you're in pretty bad shape. In fact, it seems that you're on the verge of bankruptcy."

"I realize it looks that way on paper, sir," I said. "But for the first time we feel we're on the victory side spiritually. All of us at the station have the assurance that God will pull us through."

"I'm glad you have that assurance, and glad that you've stopped cutting each other's throats over there," Mr. Beasley said, leaning back in his chair and chewing on the tip of his pencil. "But such assurances are poor collateral in a business deal. I think you ought to sweat it out."

I left his office disappointed, not realizing that God had just intervened again, closing a door in order to open a better one.

"Pat," Dede said when I walked through the back door dejected and pouring out my woeful story of failure, "there's something far bigger here than either of us realizes. Every time we've gone after the big money, God has checked us. I really believe Mr. Beasley's doing us a favor by not loaning us the money. This way we'll be forced to trust in God."

"But if God wants us to have the money, I don't see why he couldn't give it to us through Mr. Beasley," I said, slumping in a kitchen chair and running my hand through my hair.

"Because Mr. Beasley's just one man, and God wants us to have the support—and far more important, the prayers—of thousands of people."

Dede's insight into God's purpose was right. In the fall of the year we scheduled our first big telethon, hoping to raise our budget, which by then had grown to $120,000. This meant we needed to have pledges amounting to $10,000 a month, and our critics assured us that if we raised half that amount it would be a miracle. Miracles no longer bothered me; in fact, I had begun to expect them. But none of us were prepared for the immensity of the miracle about to take place.

Tony Fontaine, ex-nightclub singer and Hollywood recording star, had agreed to come with us for the weekend telethon. We were scheduled to begin with the program Saturday morning and continue through Sunday night.

Tony did a magnificent job, and by Sunday night we had been on the air almost continually. The phone calls were pouring in from all over Tidewater, but we had raised only $80,000. We were physically exhausted and resigned that we would have to settle for a budget cut of $40,000.

At 11:00 P.M. Sunday night, just before we were to sign off, Jim Bakker appeared before the camera. "Our entire purpose has been to serve the Lord Jesus Christ through radio and television," he said emotionally, his voice almost breaking. "But we've fallen short. We need $10,000 a month to stay on the air, and we're far short of that. Frankly, we're on the verge of bankruptcy and just don't have enough money to pay our bills . . ." His voice broke and he began to cry.

The cameraman in the studio held steady, his camera focused on

Jim's face as the tears rolled down and splattered on the concrete floor. Jay Arlan was sitting beside me in the darkened control booth and reached over and grabbed my arm. "Pat . . ."

I shook him off. "No," I whispered, "hold steady. God is about to do something great."

And he was. Immediately the phones in the studio started ringing until all ten lines were jammed. Those tears had touched the hearts of people all over the state. People called in, weeping.

"I want to pledge a week's salary."

"I want to pledge the money I was going to use to buy my wife an expensive Christmas present."

The wife called in. "I want to pledge the money I was going to spend on my husband."

"I had been praying for Tidewater for years but had stopped praying. I was afraid God was angry with me for having stopped, and I've asked the Lord to give me a sign that revival is about to break out. I've asked that within five minutes someone will call and pledge $500."

The moment she hung up, the phone rang again and a man said, "I want to pledge $500."

We passed midnight and went into the early morning hours as the pledging grew heavier. A young woman called in and pledged $1,000. A man called in, laughing hilariously. "I've just been waked up out of a sound sleep, and God told me to turn on the TV. I'm not giving this $100, God is."

All over Tidewater people were calling in saying that they had been waked out of deep sleep and told to turn on their TV sets. They were calling in laughing, crying, rejoicing, and praising God over the phone. By 2:30 A.M. we had raised $105,000, and we finally signed off the air. We had no further plans but to go home and praise God.

But God wasn't finished yet. The next morning the phones were ringing madly again, and all the lines were jammed. The man who had pledged $500 the night before said he didn't want to sound ostentatious on the air, but he really wanted to give $1,000. One woman called in saying, "Something is happening. I feel the holiness of God so strong from the radio that I am walking softly before the Lord in my own house."

Another woman, a schoolteacher, called and said, "One of the teachers arrived at school this morning, weeping. She's not a Christian but said as she drove across town she could sense something in the air. 'What's happening?' she asked. 'I can't understand it, but there is a presence all over Tidewater this morning. What's going on?' "

I remembered the reports I had read in the seminary of the revival in the Hebrides, and I called the staff together. "Let's go back on the air again tonight (Monday), and see what happens. Let's continue the telethon."

Monday night we were back on the air with our TV telethon, and the pledges began to come in again. By Tuesday night we had heard the command of God to tell the people that we needed to build a bigger studio and to ask men to pledge labor, mortar, bricks, and materials. All Tuesday night the phones rang, as men called to pledge their services and building materials. We were riding on the top of the clouds.

Wednesday night marked the beginning of our seventh year since we had moved to Portsmouth, and I sensed God was finally breaking through. All day long the phone had been ringing off the hook as people called in for prayer requests. One woman, the wife of one of our staff members, came crying into my office. "I've just received a message from God that we are going to be flooded with disease. Why? Why—just as we are beginning to experience revival—would God send disease upon us?"

"No, you have the wrong interpretation of that prophecy," I said gently. "God is not going to make people sick. He is going to flood us with sick people—that they may be healed."

And so it was. That night when we went on the air, our studio was filled with volunteer Christians from all over the area who were manning the battery of telephones we had installed. The calls were coming in by the hundreds as people cried out, asking for spiritual help and requesting prayer. It made no difference who answered the phone, whether it was a minister, a housewife, a bricklayer, a bookkeeper, or one of our staff. God was performing miracles.

One woman had been crippled in her legs for years, and as a young housewife prayed with her over the phone, the crippled legs were suddenly healed. I grabbed one of the ringing phones and heard a little child on the other end saying she had a terrible scar on her face and wanted me to pray that God would remove it. I prayed and hung up. Seconds later the phone rang again. It was the girl's grandmother. She was almost hysterical. "My grandchild hung up the phone and turned around and the scar, that horrible scar, was gone. It was gone! God had wiped it off her face!"

A relative of one of our employees called from New Jersey. She confessed she was an alcoholic and asked me to pray for her. I led her to Christ over the long-distance phone, and as I was witnessing to her I could hear screaming in the background. It was her sister, who finally got to the phone and said that the power of God was so strong in the room that as her sister had accepted Christ, she had been instantly healed of a painful bursitis condition in her shoulder.

John Carraway answered one of the ringing phones. It was a child in a foster home who had been watching the program and wanted to accept Christ. John led him to Jesus, and then the child asked John if he would also speak to his brothers and sisters who were in the same foster home. There were seven of them, and John led each of them to Christ, one by one. As one accepted Christ he would hand the phone to his brother until the entire family had been saved.

Hundreds of people were being ministered to for salvation. The cloud of evil that had once hovered over the station had been replaced with a cloud of righteousness, and it was as if the angels that troubled the waters at the pool of Bethesda had returned and were troubling the waters in Tidewater, only this time they did not cease. The healing and saving power remained, so that as many as wanted could come to the fountain and partake of God's grace.

Men called saying they had been sitting in front of their television sets for hours—weeping. Children were sitting glued to the sets, forgetting about the exciting network shows, entranced by the power of God. All of this was happening without any kind of programming—just the camera recording what was going on in the studio as people called in or as others came into the station to testify of what God was doing all over the city.

The revival lasted all week, and I began to realize the truth of Malachi's statement when he said, "Bring ye all the tithes into the storehouse, that there may be meat in mine house, and prove me now herewith, saith the Lord of hosts, if I will not open you the windows of heaven, and pour you out a blessing, that there shall not be room enough to receive it" (Mal. 3:10). These people had sacrificed, many of them giving out of their poverty, and now God was pouring out his blessings on those who had given. And the blessings were so great that the entire city was being overflowed by the grace of God. This was the reason God wanted many people to give, rather than just one. He wanted to pour out his blessings on many people. And he was.

The latter part of the week I received a phone call from a reporter in Newport News who asked, "What's going on over there? Do you have the Second Coming taking place? People have been calling the newspaper and saying it's the most exciting thing ever to happen in Tidewater."

"All we're doing is broadcasting from six until midnight," I said, "reading prayer requests, praying on camera, having testimonies, and announcing what God is doing."

"You mean people are getting excited about that when they could be watching 'Gunsmoke'?"

"Jesus Christ is a million times more exciting than 'Gunsmoke.'" I chuckled. "It's exciting to be present when someone is won to Christ or healed of disease. It's exciting to be present when demons are rebuked and the Holy Spirit comes in and fills a person with power and majesty. We've been on the air almost constantly, and my voice is almost gone. We have scarcely had time to eat, but praise the Lord, the blessings are coming."

"My readers might believe that a man would bite a dog," the reporter said, "but I don't think anyone would believe what you're telling me."

It made no difference. It was the sovereign work of God. It was as if Pentecost had come all over again, only this time it had come in the seventh year, the year of grace, the year of completion, the year of perfection.

XX

How Long Will You Grieve over Saul?

———
———
———

1966 was the year of the Senate Democratic primary in Virginia. Six years before, my father had won the general election with the biggest majority ever given a senatorial candidate in the history of the state. But this year things looked different. He was being opposed by a combination of blacks, young liberals, and labor coalitions. They called themselves "moderates," but actually it was the young guard versus the old guard.

Not only had my father been one of the most popular men in the state, but by virtue of his seniority he was one of the most powerful men in the Senate. He was chairman of the Senate Banking Committee, one of the ranking members of the Appropriations Committee, and floor leader for the Defense Appropriations Bill which controlled the federal budget. It was difficult to think that he could ever be beaten in his home state of Virginia.

Yet as the day of the election drew near, there was an ominous note that kept sounding in my heart. Mother had written Dad a note, warning him that if he didn't give his heart totally to Jesus Christ, he was going to be defeated. Harald Bredesen had bluntly told him the same thing: "Senator Robertson, God has invested great power in you, but if you do not return to the faith of your childhood, God will remove this power from you."

My father was a good man, a noble man, scrupulously honest, and a devoted public servant. Although he was a man of prayer, during his later years he had drifted from the earlier concepts that Jesus Christ must be total Lord of life. It was with this note of warning hanging over his head that he concluded his campaign in the primary.

His opposition lived in Portsmouth, and the local newspapers were filled with vitriolic attacks against my father. I yearned to get into the fray and start swinging, but the Lord refused to give me the liberty. "I have called you to my ministry," he spoke to my heart. "You cannot tie my eternal purposes to the success of any political candidate . . . not even your own father."

I felt I could have helped my father tremendously in the campaign, but the Lord steadfastly refused to let me. I did write one speech for him, which the newspapers said was the hardest-hitting speech of the campaign, but most of my efforts on his behalf were very frustrating.

The primary was held in July on the hottest day of the year. I drove up to his campaign headquarters in Richmond to be with him when the returns came in. But as the day wore on, something became obvious. Because of the heat, a lot of the older people who would have voted for him, simply did not turn out at the polls. The people along the coast sensed a kill and turned out in droves, while his supporters in the mountain regions and the seventh district, thinking he was strong enough to win without them, stayed away from the polls. When the final ballots were counted, some half a million votes had been cast—and he had lost by a little more than 600 votes.

I was heartbroken: for my father, for Virginia, and for the country. Even though I had not actively campaigned for him, I had lived every moment of the campaign and that night saw him, after fifty years in public office, a broken, defeated man.

Unable to bear the heartbreak any longer, Dede and I left early the next morning to drive across the states to Calgary, Alberta, Canada. The engagement had been on my calendar for several months, but now that Dad had been defeated, I hesitated.

"No," my father said, "go on. Perhaps God wants you to get away for a week so he can speak to you."

All the way across the continent I relived every detail of the primary. Our first night in Calgary, I dreamed about my father's opponent and woke early the next morning, my heart still broken. I slipped from the bed and picked up my Bible and let it fall open. As in times past, God spoke to me through the Scriptures, and this time my eyes rested on I Samuel 16:1. "How long wilt thou mourn for Saul, seeing I have rejected him from reigning over Israel? fill thine horn with oil, and go . . ."

Instantly I had peace. I knew my father's defeat was of the Lord, for his soul was far more important than his seniority in Washington. Lyndon Johnson's administration had already begun to taint the federal government with the easy morality and arrogance of the Texas wheeler-dealer. How easy for a powerful man in this environment to misuse his power. I praised God. "Thank you, Lord, for closing this door also."

But I had been beset by other problems too. In April, acting solely on faith, I had announced at a banquet that we were going to build a one-million-watt TV station. My plans were to relocate it in the central position of Tidewater in a million-dollar building. The Associated Press had picked up the story and sent it across the nation. God soon spoke to me that our plans were premature. "But what are we to do?" I argued with God. "We need the building."

"Do not rush out ahead of me," he said, "for my plans are not always your plans."

This was weighing heavily on my mind as well as the new dissensions that were brewing among the staff. I was learning that after revival the most deadly thing the devil can do is cause strife among friends. One day we would be on a spiritual mountaintop, and the next moment we'd be tearing each other up.

The meeting was at the Calgary Inn, a beautiful sumptuous hotel in the heart of Alberta. I determined I was going to seek and find the will of God for our building. Early the second morning I rose before the breakfast meeting to pray.

"Lord, what do you want me to do about this building? How are we to proceed? I'm willing to wait and follow your directions." But there was no answer.

I went to the breakfast meeting which was held in a long rectangular room. There were about 200 people present and Harald Bredesen was the only one that I knew. I arrived late. He saw me come in, and motioned me to come sit beside him in an empty chair at the head table.

The speaker that morning was a young darkheaded man I had never seen before. As he rose to speak, he suddenly turned and looked down the table where I was sitting. Since we didn't know each other, I thought little about it, but then he started in my direction. Before I had time to think, he was standing behind me, his hands on my head, prophesying.

"The Lord thy God has called thee into a great ministry. Fear not, for I will supply all your needs. You shall ride on the high places of the earth for I have heard your prayer, your conflict, your worry, and concern about this project; and I, the Lord, will build it for my glory. Do not be afraid to step out and build, for I will do it through you."

I felt the hot tears streaming down my face, for this was the answer to the prayer I had prayed so earnestly just moments before. The man returned to the speaker's stand and delivered his message. I don't remember his name, and I doubt seriously if he remembers mine. It was immaterial, however, for God had spoken.

At that same meeting, a man from California testified of how they built a building by faith for the glory of God. He said they simply called it into being. They had gone out to the building site and spoken the word of faith about the basement. They built the basement and then spoke the walls into being. They built the walls with money God provided and then, by faith, spoke the roof into being. He testified how the money, the materials, the laborers—all appeared by faith, and at last the building was erected to the glory of God. My heart sang within me.

I returned home ready to get underway. Yet, the moment we started moving out for the Lord, we came under attack again—this time from within.

Jim Bakker had been an invaluable worker. Not only had he been helping us in our telethons and the youth ministry, but had been working as a weekend radio announcer. Then one Saturday night Jay Arlan ordered him to go on the air. Jim balked, saying he was exhausted and was doing all one man could possibly do. When it came time to go on the air, he simply didn't show up.

I was out of town that weekend, and when I returned home Jay told me what had happened. I had no choice but to discipline Jim because I felt authority had to be respected.

I called Jim into my office and said, "Jim, I don't have any choice. We've established a chain of command, and you've broken it. I've got to uphold discipline and have no choice but to make you an example. Therefore I'm fining you $100."

"And I'm quitting," Jim said, turning his back and walking out.

It was an agonizing situation. I loved Jim like a brother, but knew that I had to uphold discipline or the whole station would become an anarchy.

The next morning, after I finished my radio program, "Powertime," I started out of the studio when I heard the voice of God: "Don't fire Jim Bakker."

I called John Stallings to ask his advice. "God is dealing with me to keep Jim. What do I do?"

"You do what God tells you to do, regardless," he answered.

"How can I do that when Jim's defied orders?"

"I don't know, but if God said so, then you better find some way to bring him back into the fold."

"Now look, John. I've given a directive, and if I don't stick to it, we're going to be in real trouble. I've got to uphold that fine. Besides, I've already contacted a man about replacing Jim."

"I think you better do a lot of praying before you make any sudden moves," John said.

But I had already made a sudden move. That afternoon I had phoned a husband and wife team who had previously applied for a job. He lived in Ohio and came highly recommended. "Come right away," I had said.

Thursday morning I was sitting at my desk when Jim Bakker walked back into the station. His face showed he had spent several sleepless nights, and his eyes were red from weeping. "God has really been dealing with me," he said. "I don't think I should leave. I feel that God wants me here. I've never been more miserable in all my life, and I want to come back."

"Well, I'm delighted to have you back, but we still have to do something about this fine," I said.

"Pat, I just don't have the money. I guess that's one of the reasons I walked out. It was easier to quit than to admit I was broke."

"I think we should pray," I said, remembering John Stallings' words. "Maybe if we had done this earlier, we wouldn't be in this spot now."

I had levied the fine, and the staff expected me to make it stick; yet God had told me not to fire Jim (even if he didn't pay the fine). So I finally gave the $100 to Jim, and he paid the fine, to the satisfaction of the staff. None of them knew the fine was paid with my money.

Now I was faced with an even greater problem. The couple from Ohio were due in that afternoon—the ones I had hired to replace Jim and Tammy.

"Be calm in your soul," I heard God whispering to me as I bowed my head in prayer. "I have a plan for this also."

Ronnie Poole arrived that afternoon with his wife, and I called him into my office, giving him the full story. "I know we've brought you all the way from Ohio," I apologized, "but we just don't have a place for you now that Jim is back with us."

He leaned back in his chair and sighed. "Thank you, God," he prayed out loud. "You know I really didn't want to go into television work. You know that what I really want to do is build buildings and . . ."

"You're a builder?" I shouted, interrupting his prayer.

"Yes," he said half-ashamed. "I didn't tell you that because my wife and I love work with children. That's the reason we were willing to go into television and radio."

"Praise the Lord," I said hurrying around the desk and shaking his hand. "That's what God has been trying to say to me all along. We're getting ready to build a new station and have been through eight sets of plans from the architect and not one of them has been able to give us satisfaction."

"Let me look at your plans," he said. "God has been showing me some methods of construction using prefab metal buildings where you can get a lot of space very cheaply."

Ronnie Poole shared his concepts with us, and the following Saturday morning I sat down at my dining-room table and sketched out the building plans, using his ideas. Everything appeared before me as I sketched: halls, offices, prayer room, and two huge studios. Ronnie returned to Ohio, and we made plans to break ground for our new Radio and Television Broadcasting Center.

The next week God spoke through Jim Bakker, of all people, with a prophecy in our staff meeting: "I want to bring you to the higher ground, but you always keep coming back to the same point. Move on. I want to lead you to better things, yet I cannot because you continually come back to the same point in your inability to get along with each other. Thus I must deal with you here and not let you into the area where I want to give you a ministry. I am calling you to unity. Therefore, be all together in one place, and I shall pour out again my spirit of Pentecost."

XXI

The Miracle-Worker

———
———
———

The highlights of our years were becoming the fall telethons. In 1966 we invited Stuart Hamblen to come as our featured entertainer for the weekend. Three days prior to the beginning of the telethon, we had a prayer meeting with the staff, and God gave me a word of prophecy. He said, "I am ready to harvest the people and am going to do greater things than you have ever seen before."

It was hard for me to believe, even though the words had come out of my own mouth. How could God do a greater thing than he had done the year before?

We began the telethon at 3:00 P.M. on Friday. The staff was gathered on benches in the studio for prayer. Dede was with me, and there was a great feeling of excitement. "Don't you realize what is about to happen, Pat?"

"I wish I did," I said.

"Last year the people pledged so generously, and because of it, all this year God has prospered them. Just wait; as soon as we go on the air, God is going to bless beyond measure as the people start pledging out of their new prosperity."

Dede was right. We were not only going to oversubscribe our budget of $150,000, but would raise an additional $30,000 to purchase a new transmitter. However, the greatest victory would come in another area.

Beginning Friday night we were flooded with telephone calls and prayer requests. We had installed twelve telephones, and they were tied up almost around the clock, with thousands of prayer requests coming in.

At 10:30 P.M. an eighty-four-year-old man called the station. He said he had been blind for three years and wanted us to pray that he would receive his sight. His name was included in about twenty other prayer requests, all of which were shared on the air. The next morning the man's landlady came in to wake him. She shook him gently and he turned over, opened his eyes, and stared at her.

"You can see!" she whispered, unbelievingly.

"Yes," he said with a shaky voice, his eyes riveted on her face. "Praise God, I can see."

"Am I beautiful?" the sixty-five-year-old woman asked.

"Yes," he said, his voice trembling with excitement. "You are the most beautiful thing I have ever seen."

That was the beginning of things. There were literally hundreds of dramatic answers to prayer. The phones were manned by volunteers who came in to pray for those in need and to witness to those who wanted to accept Christ. Almost as a sideline, they accepted pledges toward the monetary goal.

One little housewife, Delores Johnson, a twenty-four-year-old member of a Baptist church, was beside herself. Every time she prayed over the phone there was an instantaneous answer to the prayer. "In the name of Jesus," she would almost shout over the phone. She prayed for one woman who had a great swelling in her legs, and as she prayed, the swelling went down. All over the studio we could hear the healed woman as she screamed with joy on the other end of the phone line.

All this was on live TV. By now we had two cameras, one focused on the bank of phones and the other on the MC. As phone calls came in and prayers were answered, the MC would take the mike to the man or woman who had answered the call. "Praise the Lord, a man and his wife were just saved." Occasionally the camera would focus on the big thermometer that showed the amount of pledges, but by and large the excitement was not in raising money, but in the spiritual victories.

Sometimes the power of God was so strong that it would actually knock the people back from the phone receiver on the other end as our people prayed for them. I answered one phone and the man on the other end was in tears, begging with me to pray that he could be delivered from cigarette smoking. As I prayed, the power of God came upon him and knocked him back. He literally reeled away from the phone—delivered.

Saturday night a woman came into the studio with arthritis of the spine. We prayed for her in front of the camera and God healed her. At the same time, a woman listening to the simulcast by radio fifty miles away was instantly healed of the same condition.

Sunday afternoon a mother called in asking that we pray for her six-week-old baby who had been born with a twisted foot. The baby was scheduled for an operation the next week. Five minutes after we prayed, the father called back. He said he was a member of a Free Will Baptist Church in Newport News and thought this whole program was fanatical, but as we prayed for his daughter, before his very eyes, the twisted foot had straightened out, and the baby was completely whole. He was weeping and praising God over the phone.

By Sunday night we had raised our $150,000 and gone on to raise the additional money for the transmitter. These were just like days in heaven, and it seemed wrong to get back to any kind of regular programming. Yet we knew we couldn't keep on with this pace indefinitely. We met Monday afternoon in prayer, and every one of us received the witness that God wanted the program to continue each night. Since we had begun our telethons calling them "The 700 Club Telethon," we decided to call the nightly program the "700 Club Program."

Beginning that night, we came on at ten o'clock. Since this was a team effort, there were usually two co-hosts plus dedicated workers sitting behind a bank of telephones. Prayer and praise was at the heart of the program. Our theme Scripture was Matthew 18:19: "If two of you shall agree on earth as touching anything that they shall ask, it shall be done for them of my Father which is in heaven."

Now we finally had God's program. There was a total involvement with our audience. The program was simulcast on radio and television. Those with spiritual, physical, or other needs could call in their requests, and as they did, the phones ringing in the background would be heard on the air. When the requests were shared with the audience, the people could pray for one another. When an answer to prayer was reported or someone was led to Christ on the telephone, the audience could rejoice together.

We were completely free in the Spirit. Although there were guests for interviews and music, there was no script. If God said sing, we sang. If he said give an invitation, we gave it. If he said interview a guest, we interviewed the guest. And best of all, there was no time limit. Since this was the last program of the day, we could stay on until three o'clock in the morning if God was touching people's lives. If nothing seemed to be happening, we could sign the station off the air and go to bed.

One night Jim Bakker was the host of the "700 Club Program." He had enjoyed a good night, but when midnight came he signaled for sign-off. The count down to sign off was underway and less than sixty seconds remained when God spoke to him: "You have not drawn the net."

In an instant Jim realized what had happened. During the program his words had awakened a desire for salvation in the hearts of the viewers, but he had not followed up with an invitation.

"We can't go off yet," he shouted to the director, the audience, and anybody else who happened to be listening. "Hold the sign-off. God isn't finished."

With that he proceeded to give a simple invitation to those who wanted to accept Christ. Eleven people responded, and then the Lord said, "Now you can go home."

Sometimes we tried to draw the net too quickly. One night after the program had been on for an hour, I began to give an invitation for members of the audience to accept Christ. After the third sentence God spoke, "This is not the time."

I stopped short, stammered once or twice, then continued, "Yes friends, it is a great life; and now to sing about it, here are the Downings."

We had some young people with us that night who had been singing and testifying of their faith. They sang once more, and as they did I was so filled with God's power that I could hardly breathe. When they finished, I was back on the air. "Now," God said.

At that moment I led in prayer all those in the audience who wanted to take Jesus Christ as their Savior. Then I asked all those who had prayed with me to call in. The phones literally exploded. People were weeping and laughing. One college boy said that he had been high on drugs every day for the past year, and now he was saved. A girl who had been living with the hippies for three years said she had given her heart to Jesus and was going home to her family. Little children were calling, along with people in their eighties. I could hardly talk. All we could do was report what God was doing.

The "700 Club Program" obviously had universal appeal. When you pray for people, you make friends. It makes no difference who they are: Protestants, Catholics, Jews, Buddhists, even Atheists—all are grateful that you care enough to pray. Since God was answering prayer, the word spread widely that if anybody in Tidewater needed help, they could get it at CBN. It wasn't long before we were receiving tens of thousands of prayer requests and had expanded our on-the-air intercession on radio to include prayer time at 4:00, 7:30, and 9:30 in the morning, 12:00 noon, and 3:30 in the afternoon. Coupled with the "700 Club Program" and our regular staff prayer meeting, we were interceding twenty-four hours a day.

My mind flashed back through the years to an afternoon spent in the Classan Avenue Presbyterian Church in Brooklyn. As I knelt at the front of the old church, God had spoken to me: "I have called you to be an intercessor." Now that intercessory prayer was at the very heart of our ministry, I finally understood what he had been talking about.

With the establishment of the "700 Club" as a nightly feature, I got back to work trying to raise the money for a loan at the bank to finance our new building. However, our auditor was overworked, and the days went by and we still didn't have the financial statement necessary to show the bank. I grew impatient and did everything I could to speed him up, but he was just slow—maddeningly slow!

When I finally got the balance sheets, I rushed them down to the Citizens Trust Company in Portsmouth to apply for our loan.

I later learned that on this very afternoon the Federal Reserve Board had met in Washington and lowered the amount of reserves required to be kept by member banks. This simple action made millions of dollars available for banks to loan. Tidewater banks were in a position to make substantial loans to borrowers they could not have considered the day before. God had used our "slow" auditor to put us first in line for the new money.

Six years before we had been turned down for a $5,000 loan because we were not a "bankable proposition." Now without hesitation the Citizen's Trust Company gave the green light for a loan of $225,000 on our new building.

Paul Morris came down and we broke ground for the new station on June 5, 1967—the same day the Jews went to war with the Arabs at the beginning of the Six-Day War in Israel. The Scripture I read that morning was from Luke 21:24. ". . . and Jerusalem shall be trodden down of the Gentiles, until the times of the Gentiles be fulfilled."

We were under construction throughout that summer and into the fall. We had hoped to be finished in time for our fall telethon, but construction was slow, and there was dust and filth and water everywhere as we tried the best we could to carry on normal broadcasting. One day, while I was on camera, a piece of the new roof opened up and a column of water descended between me and the camera. Another time the Cameron Family from Scotland had come into the studio to sing. They were dressed in their kilts and skirts, and as they sang, there was an anointing of the Spirit, and they began to dance around the studio. All was well, except they raised so much dust some of our viewers thought it was the charge of the Light Brigade.

Ronnie Avalone, one of the world's greatest dramatic tenors, and Dale Evans, wife of Roy Rogers, came with us for the telethon that fall. We opened with a concert in Norfolk and filled up two auditoriums, before moving to the studio. We intended to run the telethon all week, expecting it to take us that long to raise our budget of $240,000. However, by Tuesday night we had reached the budget, Ronnie and Dale had left, and suddenly we didn't know what to do with the rest of the week.

Caught unprepared for such a quick victory, we retreated rather than advancing and immediately felt the anointing of God leave. By Friday night the entire staff was disgusted with each other, right on the heels of the greatest financial victory the station had ever had.

At five the next afternoon I asked those who were supposed to be on the air that night to gather with me in the prayer room. We held hands in unity and asked God to pour out his power upon us. We left and went into the new studio which was almost completed.

Immediately we realized God had given us victory as we prayed. That night and on into the next day we counted twenty-five people who were instantly healed of deafness. Jim Bakker prayed for a little boy who had crossed eyes, and his eyes were straightened instantly. But the climax came that Saturday night.

Harry Van Deventer was a blind man who had been playing the piano for us. He had become a usual figure around the studio, tapping with his white cane. During the 700 Club program that night, Harry got up from the piano and tapped his way out into the middle of the studio in front of the camera and said, "I feel the anointing of the Lord so great in this room. Will you pray for me?"

I asked the entire crew to join me as we prayed. Even the cameramen locked their cameras on automatic and walked around in front to lay hands on Harry. Three times we prayed, and then he opened his eyes and began looking around. He first looked up at the bright lights and then at the faces of those standing and kneeling around him, and he began to weep. "I can see!" he shouted at the camera. "I can see!"

He let his white cane fall to the floor and nimbly walked back across the studio. Stepping easily over all the cables that snaked their way across the floor, he sat down at the piano. The camera swung and picked him up as he said softly, "God has given me a song, and tonight I want to play it. It's called, 'The Miracle Worker.' "

The power of the Lord was there as Harry played and sang about the One who makes the lame to walk and the blind to see.

XXII

New Continents for Christ

Back in 1963, when we were having such a hard financial struggle, I had been led to take a thousand dollars from the proceeds of a loan and send it to a missionary in Korea named Dove Toll. I had been in seminary with Dove and was impressed with her desire to go to Korea and train Koreans to be missionaries to other countries.

Dove, in turn, gave the thousand dollars to a Mrs. Lea who was going as a missionary from Korea to Bolivia. Dove wrote me and mentioned in her letter that many years before, Mrs. Lea had visited in Norfolk as the guest of an eighty-year-old retired Methodist missionary. The Methodist missionary had shared with Mrs. Lea her heavy burden to pray for a Christian television station in Tidewater. Mrs. Lea had promised to join her in prayer, and all these years had been praying for God to open a Christian TV station in Tidewater. Dove concluded her letter saying, "Mrs. Lea never understood why God placed such a burden on her heart to pray for a television station in such a faraway place. But now she knows. She has cast her bread upon the waters and after many days it has returned to her."

Because of this, we had developed an intense interest in missions, and each year had given money from the station to further the kingdom of God in some faraway place. This year (1967) we had sent $5,000 to Elim Bible Institute in New York telling them to use it in their missionary offering. A portion of the money had gone to a former missionary to Cuba, Sixto Lopez, who now had a radio ministry in Bogota, Colombia.

In May I had spent three days in prayer at home—fasting, praying, and seeking God's direction. One of my prayer burdens concerned a letter I had received from Sixto. It was a routine missionary letter, but at the bottom he had penned a P.S. "More than 600 people have received the baptism in the Holy Spirit during the last few weeks. Now the radio station where I have my program is for sale. Would you be interested in it?"

Like the P.S. on the bottom of George Lauderdale's letter, this one also seemed to carry the prophetic anointing of God.

That summer I met Sixto in New York at a meeting with Harald Bredesen. Sixto kept saying, "You and Harald must come to Bogota."

Therefore, prior to our telethon in the fall of 1967 I flew to Bogota, and Harald later joined me, along with two Spirit-filled Catholic priests. I immediately fell in love with the "air-conditioned city." The Colombian people were so gracious, and I sensed the sweetness of spirit that radiated from these people who had been under great religious persecution for so many years. In fact, in the outlying provinces, the missionaries were still being stoned for preaching Jesus.

But the most thrilling aspect of all was the challenge. It was God's timing. Pope John and the Ecumenical Council had opened a new era of understanding between Catholics and Protestants. The Catholic Church in Colombia was completely willing for us to purchase a radio station which would broadcast the Gospel to this city of 2½ million people. This was made clear when Harald and his two Spirit-filled priests visited the Archbishop of Colombia. The archbishop embraced Harald and called him "my brother in Christ," kissing him on both cheeks. He even went further, inviting him and his two Pentecostal priests to speak in the Catholic universities. We knew that the time was ripe for God to move in Colombia.

But there were problems. The station was owned by a Señor Espitia who was a petty bandito with slicked-down hair and a pencil-thin moustache. Espitia was demanding 950,000 pesos, or about $53,000. We negotiated, but were unable to reach any settlement. It was obvi-

ous this little Colombian had his eye on the rich American's dollars
and was out to take us for all he could. Not only that, but we found
out that the lawyer who was supposed to be representing us was a
double agent, being paid a retainer by Espitia as well. However, we
finally reached a settlement and agreed to give him $5,000 down
payment at the signing of a contract.

Since the contracts were all written in Spanish, I had to depend on
our lawyer to make sure everything was legal. Therefore, it wasn't
until the next day that I discovered we had acted in haste. The contract could be a trap. We would be obligated to pay for the station
even if the government did not authorize the transfer of the station
license. If Espitia ever realized that this loophole was in the contract,
he could simply keep our money and stall the proceedings before the
Ministry of Communications.

Sixto and I took a long walk that morning. The temperature in Bogota is fifty-eight degrees year-round, but the altitude is 8,600 feet,
and being accustomed to walking around at sea level, I took a while
to catch my breath. We climbed up to a knoll overlooking the city.
After I caught my breath, I began to pray. God gave me an utterance
in tongues, followed by prophecy in which he assured us of absolute
victory. "I have given you this city, and I have called you to come in
and possess the land. I will go ahead of you and take care of you and
will handle all the negotiations. The victory is mine."

We left that beautiful point and returned to the city, meeting with
the lawyers and Senor Espitia in the posh dining room of the Continental Hotel. After dinner I recited the things I wanted, and held my
breath.

Instead of Espitia's expected wrangling, he meekly consented to
all my changes in the contract, and not only that, gave us terms even
more favorable than we dared ask for. Either he was a lot less shrewd
than we had taken him for, or God had gone ahead of us, blocked his
consciousness, and changed his mind.

In any event, we redrafted the contract on our terms and agreed to a fifty-fifty relationship in the station for a six-month period beginning in February 1968. Now all I had to do was return to Portsmouth and raise $25,000.

We went on the air with the telethon called "New Continents for Christ," stating that if we purchased the station we would call it *Nuevo Continente*—New Continent for Christ. I told the television audience of our burden for missions and asked them to join me in believing that God would supply the needed $25,000.

We set up our battery of telephones from the "700 Club" and started taking pledges along with prayer requests. By the end of the week, it was obvious that God was going to provide the money necessary to purchase the station. It was about 10:30 Sunday night when we went over the top. Jim Bakker shouted, "We've done it! We're over the goal! We've raised the money for *Nuevo Continente!*"

Just as he made his announcement, there was a horrible noise on the roof. A violent gust of wind from the ocean had picked up the roofing of the unfinished studio and rolled it back across our heads like it was a sheet of tissue paper. Then a section of the roof decking crashed onto the studio floor. Overhead we could see the stars.

I was kneeling behind one of the sets talking on the phone to a man who was about to accept Christ when the accident occurred. I looked up at Jim, and his eyes were as big as saucers. He screamed into the camera, "Everybody run for your lives, the roof's falling in."

The women at the telephone table were screaming and running in all directions, tripping over the phone wires. I was shouting, "Wait, wait!" to those in the studio and at the same time trying to encourage the man on the phone to "go ahead" and make his decision. Jim was shouting, "It's an explosion from the devil to show his displeasure that we're moving into Bogota."

Suddenly we were off the air, in one of the most climactic program endings in the annals of television.

XXIII

To Claim a World

———
———
———

Mother died Wednesday after Easter. Dede and I had driven up to Lexington on Good Friday and that night had stood out in the yard looking at what was known as a "blood moon," a partial eclipse that showed a reddish tinge so it looked like blood on the moon.

"The Bible says that blood on the moon is a sure sign of the near return of the Lord," Mother had said. "Wouldn't it be wonderful if He would return tonight—or on Easter morning?"

We stood in the yard a long time, talking about the coming of the Lord and enjoying a sweet feeling of fellowship. We returned to Portsmouth Sunday afternoon and Tuesday Mother called, saying she had had some heart trouble and wanted me to pray for her. I did, and then pleaded with her to see a doctor since she was at home by herself. I called her back the next day and again asked her to see a doctor, and although she said she preferred to be at home by herself, she agreed to call one and let him come by and examine her.

An hour and a half later, when the doctor arrived, he found her. "There was a magnificent radiance on her face and surrounding her body," he later told me, "but her spirit was gone."

Her passing was an emotional shock to me, and since I was already exhausted trying to get the building ready for its official opening, I felt I was about to collapse. During this emotional depression, the staff gathered in our new office for a prayer time. It was just a week before the building was to be dedicated. As we prayed, a great spirit of confession and weeping fell on the room. Suddenly the weariness was lifted, and I heard myself praying with great power. I began to pray for the $200,000 we needed to finish paying for the building, but the Holy Spirit checked me and said, "I want you to pray for the world."

Instantly, as if He had reached His hand into my heart and enlarged it, I felt the capacity to accommodate a vision far greater than I had ever had before. I knew this was Mother's dream, to evangelize the world for Jesus, and suddenly it became my vision too. "I want you to claim the world for Jesus," the Holy Spirit was directing. I heard myself praying with great power, and felt an enormous faith building in my heart that the entire world could, indeed, hear the good news of Jesus. It was not an impossible task—just a difficult one—and God was calling me to help bring it to pass.

We dedicated our new building on May 3 with an open house. More than 11,000 people came by to see the new station facilities, and we prayed the same prayer Solomon prayed when he dedicated the Temple, asking God to place His holiness in the station and to come down and dwell in it. The beautiful prayer chapel was dedicated to the memory of my mother. Located just to the right of the front entrance, the chapel was alive with symbolic meaning. Everything in the room forced attention heavenward. A hand-carved cross was suspended in the middle of the room over an uncut boulder of white crystal rock. There was no pulpit, only three concentric rows of circular benches ringing the central point so that all who entered would know that Christ was the center, the rock upon which CBN rested.

Sunday night is normally a quiet time. We're not on the air since we haven't wanted to run in competition with the various churches. But the weekend of the grand opening we felt a strong compulsion to stay on the air and broadcast Sunday night as well. That night I gave a Gospel invitation, asking anybody who wanted to accept the Lord to call the station. We had only four telephone lines open at the time but instantly all of them were jammed with incoming calls. The calls came in so fast we had to ask the audience to be patient, assuring them that we would get to them as soon as possible. That night more than 100 people gave their hearts to Christ over the phone.

The tremendous flow of the Spirit of God continued the next night, and once again, without any pressure, a hundred more people were led to the Lord. The phones rang for six solid hours, and 50 percent of those calling were teenagers. By the end of the week, more than 500 had called to register their first-time decisions for the Lord.

Tuesday night, at 11:30, the holiness of God came into the new studio in such an awesome way that Jim Bakker, who was on the air, suddenly said, "We are on holy ground here in the studio, and we'll have to take off our shoes."

I looked around, and everyone in the studio was taking off his shoes. Jim was right. The glory of the Lord was filling the room, and I, too, took off my shoes. Jim handed me the microphone. "I'm going to pray," he said, and stepped over to one side and began to praise the Lord. Left before the camera with my shoes off and holding the mike, I heard God's voice saying to me, "Pat, get out of the way."

"God, where can I go? I'm in front of the camera."

"Just get out of the way so the people can see me," he said.

I glanced at Jim Bakker. He was on his knees, his hands raised, and his face upturned to heaven. I tried to get him to come back on camera, but he wasn't there. His spirit had been transported to the heavenlies, and he kept saying, "I don't want to come back. I don't want to come back."

Tammy, down at the other end of the studio, began to get happy in the Lord and was virtually screaming with joy. I just looked at the camera and said, "God told me to get out of the way, and I don't know what to do or where to go. I just don't want to block his power."

Lee Russell, a fine singer, was in the studio. I turned to him and said, "Brother, sing something so I can get out of the way."

Lee began to sing, and the anointing of the Holy Spirit was so intense in the room that one of the cameramen put his arm up over the camera and began to weep uncontrollably until there was a pool of water, a puddle, under his feet. We stayed on the air until 2:30 A.M., praising God and answering the phone as people called in and told of wonderful miracles that had happened as they were watching.

It was the beginning of a new era with us, and slowly, as the summer wore on, I began to understand the burden God had put on my heart for winning the world to Christ.

Our first step, of course, was the station in Colombia. We determined to have a summer telethon, calling it "Crisis Year—1968." We went on the air asking people to share in this ministry of worldwide missions. For fifty nonstop hours we were on the air with a marathon telethon. When we finished, I felt my brain had been burned into my head from the bright lights of the studio, but the burden was being shared by thousands who had begun to pray for an entire world.

The next week I took Henry Harrison, a veteran of nearly twenty years of radio who had joined us as radio station manager of WXRI-FM, and we flew to Bogota to meet with Sixto Lopez to begin on July 15, 100 percent operation of station *Nuevo Continente* in Colombia. The station had been running thirty-six beer commercials a day from the Bavarian Beer Industry, which is the biggest corporation in Colombia. Their contract ran out in August, and some of the people in Bogota thought we should keep the commercials until then. I said absolutely not, and we dropped all the beer commercials the day we took over.

Not only did we drop the beer commercials, but we also dropped the lottery and cigarette commercials, which meant that the first day we lost more than half our advertising income. Besides this, we had made the ad agencies mad for dropping the beer commercials, and they indicated they just wouldn't be very cooperative in giving us any ads in the future. So, we opened the station with two strikes against us.

The day before we took over, Henry Harrison, Sixto, and I drove to a little watering hole down the road from Bogota and went swimming. We swam and prayed and asked the Lord for the right name for our program which would be similar to the "700 Club" where the Colombian people would call in and request prayer. As we praised God there in the beautiful outdoor setting, Sixto said, "This is so beautiful. It is a 'momentos de gozo y allevanza.' "

"What's that?" I asked Sixto.

"That means 'moments of joy and praise.' "

"That's it!" I said. "That's what we'll call our program."

That night, Henry, Sixto, Oscar Rodriguez (a Methodist missionary), and I went up to the station at nine o'clock. We raised our hands and walked about the station claiming it for Jesus and saying, "Momentos de gozo y allevanza."

The station was on the air, and the response was instant. People who had never heard gospel hymns before started calling in their requests and asking for prayer. The next night, volunteer workers, including Sixto's dedicated wife, came to the studio to answer the phone while Sixto conducted the program. As the days went by, people began writing in from all over Colombia. Letters came even from Equador, Peru, and Venezuela as men and women, for the first time, heard the Gospel message and called asking how they could be saved. A call came from the nuns at a Catholic convent, asking us to pray for a sick priest and thanking us for the beautiful music. God had given us a toehold on the world.

Bogota was just the beginning. On my return to Portsmouth from my first trip to Bogota, I had learned that Channel 46 in Atlanta was open. A group called Delta Communications had requested it from the FCC but had been turned down. Now they were applying again. Atlanta was one of the cities we had on our Master Plan which we had been praying about for years. Now it seemed God might be opening the door.

I conferred with our FCC attorney, and we submitted an application to the FCC for Channel 46. It wasn't long before the lawyer called me back and said, "Either you're awful lucky or the Lord is with you, because your opponents in this thing have dropped out of the race."

"I'm not so lucky, but the Lord is with me," I laughed.

Within weeks, the FCC had granted us a permit to begin operating a UHF television station in Atlanta under Channel 46. Much local interest was shown and plans were made to build a 1,800,000-watt station to broadcast in full color. The dream we had had for so many years was beginning to take on some form and substance. However, before that dream would fully materialize, there would be another man to enter the picture who would make a profound impact on CBN.

I first met Scott Ross when I spoke at a Full Gospel Business Men's meeting in Baltimore in the summer of 1968. At the close of the meeting this long-haired, moustached young man came up to speak to me. Despite the fact that he was dressed in a wild psychedelic shirt with tight pants and boots, I liked the sparkle in his eyes and the contagious smile he flashed through his moustache. He introduced himself as Scott Ross and said he was a radio announcer who had accepted Jesus Christ and been baptized in the Holy Spirit just a short time before.

I liked him immediately and later in the summer contacted him, asking him if he would like to go to work for us, directing programs toward teenagers.

"Sure," he said when I called him, "but maybe you should check me out first."

I followed through on his references, and what I learned almost "blew my mind." Scott had come out of a heavy drug culture in New York and had turned to Jesus in a big way. At one time he was the youngest disc jockey in the Long Island area and had emceed the concerts of various acid-rock groups such as the Beatles and the Rolling Stones. In fact, it was with the Rolling Stones that he smoked most of his marijuana, and later, rooming with a hard rock group called The Lost Souls, he had taken huge overdoses of LSD.

None of this bothered me, because I recognized the real quality of his present life. I felt he was just the man to share the Gospel with an upbeat generation of kids who were turning on to drugs rather than turning their lives over to Jesus.

The last reference I talked to was the pastor of the church where Scott had been saved. "I think there is one other thing you should know about him," the pastor said after giving him the highest recommendation.

"What is that?"

"Well, he is married to a Negro girl."

My heart did a flip-flop. Here I was, dependent on the conservative Christians of the Tidewater area for our support, and getting ready to bring in a hippie-type disc jockey with a black wife. Without wanting it, I realized I was on the spot.

"So, what are you going to do?" Dede chided me.

I knew what I was going to do; it's just that it was hard to do it. I prayed, "Lord, I want to reach these young people for Jesus, and I believe Scott Ross is the right man. I also believe that you've put your approval on his marriage. Now if that means this is going to tear down my entire ministry, I can't help it. I'm willing to take the chance." In essence, I was laying the entire ministry of CBN on the line by inviting Scott and his beautiful bride, the former Nedra Talley, to join us.

Nedra had sung with a group called the Ronettes. They had toured Europe and the United States, had toured with the Beatles and sold more than 4 million records. Her weekly income had been $1,500 on nightclub engagements, but she had given all this up to accept Christ and marry Scott.

It turned out she was a perfectly charming person with rather light-colored skin, something that was to stand in her favor in those early days in Portsmouth.

"Are you a mulatto?" the landlord asked sheepishly when Scott and Nedra went out to look at a house.

"Certainly not!" Nedra said tersely.

The landlord was embarrassed and said, "I'm sorry. It's just that your skin is dark, and we don't want any niggers living in this area."

Scott and Nedra knew they would have to face people like this, so they simply praised God and moved in. However, it wasn't the race issue that made Scott a controversial figure, it was his radical ideas for reaching young people for Jesus.

"Man, we've gotta go where they're at," Scott told me when he outlined his plans to play gospel rock music over WXRI-FM. "These dudes on the beach aren't going to listen to the Haven of Rest Quartette when they're groovin' on the Jefferson Airplane and the Beatles. You've gotta start where they are and bring them up to where we are."

I knew Scott was right, but I also knew that most of our listeners would disagree—violently. In fact, even some of our own staff members who were on radio and TV were making statements like, "I can't go along with all this rock music. Let's face it. That beat is of the devil." And most of our listeners agreed.

Thus, realizing that we were never going to reach today's youth with a bland diet of milk and crackers, I told Scott to follow the leading of the Lord and go ahead and spice things up, even if we lost our heads. And we almost did.

One of Scott's first brainstorms was to go out and bring in a shaggy rock combo from the drug scene on Virginia Beach and put them on TV. His plan was to allow these dirty, long-haired musicians to appear in the studio and have the camera pan their sad faces one by one as they played. Then Scott would come on and say, "Does God love these people?" Then they would hit the music loud and heavy, and Scott would keep breaking in with the Gospel message, speaking to the kids in language they could understand.

To put it mildly, it was a radical departure from the usual program produced by CBN, and our staff reacted with vehemence, especially when some of the boys were seen taking dope in the back part of the studio before their performance.

"To think they would allow this to go on in God's house," one sec-

retary snorted as she saw the scraggly group of "drug freaks" standing before the camera twanging away with their loud music.

"You're living in the dark ages, Honey," Scott said as he overheard
the remark. "It's time to take a trip on Jesus and get turned on to the
Holy Spirit. That's where it's at."

The tension was so thick you could almost see it crackle in the air.
I bowed my head and prayed God would bring some kind of order
out of the seeming chaos that was taking place.

The order came, just as God wanted it. John Gimenez, former
New York drug addict and now pastor of the Rock Church in Virginia Beach, had been part of Scott's program. Afterward he and
Scott took the youths into the prayer room for a prayer meeting. Several of the staff joined them, and almost immediately the power of
God swept across the room and there was singing in the Spirit,
prophecy, tongues, and interpretation. The shaggy, barefooted musicians were looking around, wide-eyed and filled with wonder. No
doubt they thought some of their companions were weird when they
were freaked out on drugs, but this was something else.

Gimenez and Scott were kneeling on the floor, calling out to God
in loud voices when Gimenez unexpectedly got up from his knees
and walked over to where one of the youths was sitting. "I believe
this young man wants to be saved," John said. Kneeling before him,
he began to pray, and then quietly presented the plan of salvation.

"Do you want to accept Jesus Christ as your Savior?" John said.

The kinky-headed boy dropped his head and fingered the beads
around his neck. Looking up he said, "I . . . I . . ." and broke into
tears, grabbing John around the neck and burying his bearded face in
his shoulder.

"Praise the Lord," Scott shouted, and moved over to where the
other youths were seated on the benches. "God loves you, and we
love you," he said. And even some of those who had been most ada-
mant against these hippies came over and knelt with him as they
prayed for the rest. It was a much-needed lesson in love and compassion.

But even after this breakthrough, Scott's problems in Portsmouth continued to mount. Many of our listeners were offended by his up-beat tempo music as well as by his radical mode of dress. It was obvious that something was going to have to give, although I was determined to keep him on our staff because of his valuable contribution to the ministry.

The problem came to a sudden head when some of Nedra's relatives came to visit her. Unlike Nedra, they were dark-skinned—very dark.

"I thought you said you weren't mulatto," the landlord said when he came to complain.

"I'm not," Nedra smiled. "My father is an Indian."

"I'm sorry to have to do this," he said sheepishly, "but we're going to have to ask you to leave."

"Why?" Nedra said, never losing her poise.

"This sounds strange, I know," the landlord said, fumbling for words, "but having black children playing on the street offends the people coming home from church on Sunday."

"Then we'll leave," Nedra said sweetly. "If there's one group we don't want to offend, it's church people."

But it was God's timing, for while this was going on the Holy Spirit had been working out another set of circumstances to mesh with Scott's expulsion from Portsmouth—circumstances that would thrust us into an entirely new phase of ministry.

Just before I had left for Bogota on my last trip, I had interviewed a man by the name of Andy Andersen who was applying for a job as newscaster with WXRI-TV. Andy had been working for a chain of radio stations in upper New York state called Northeast Radio Network—five interconnected stations with headquarters in Ithaca, reaching Buffalo, Rochester, Albany, and Syracuse.

I wanted to hire Andy, but in our conversation he kept talking about this tremendous setup of interconnected Class B FM stations, whereby the Ithaca station did all the programming and then sent it out for the other stations to run simultaneously. The stations had been owned by the C & U Telephone Company, which had just been bought out by the Continental Telephone Company in St. Louis. I wasn't particularly interested in owning five FM stations in New York, and promptly forgot about the matter.

A few days later I received a phone call from a man named Joe Sitrick, a broker with Blackburn and Company which is the largest radio and TV broker in America. Strick said he had heard from Andy Andersen that we might be interested in purchasing these radio stations.

"I told Andy that I wasn't interested," I said, slightly miffed. "I guess he misunderstood me."

"The stations are worth $600,000," Sitrick said, "but I think they can be purchased for half that amount."

"Brother, we don't any more have $300,000 than we have a TV tower on the moon," I said.

"Well, think the matter over and give me a call later in the week," the broker said.

I did think it over—and prayed it over. A week later I called Sitrick back and made him a proposition. "If you can work out a deal where the Continental Telephone Company will *give* us the stations, we'll give them a tax-deductible receipt for their market value of $600,000 and we'll guarantee you a cash commission of 5 percent on the original offer of $300,000."

Sitrick said, "I'll take it back to them and see what they'll do."

It was then that an amazing chain of events rapidly began to develop. Totally unknown to me, the Comptroller of Continental Telephone Company was a man named Brucker Arnold, who just happened to be the brother-in-law of Neil Eskelin, our first program director. When the proposal from the broker crossed his desk he said, "Oh yes, I know all about CBN. My brother-in-law used to work for them. They're a fine organization, and I think this is a good deal for our company. I approve it."

On the recommendation of the broker and the Comptroller, the

Board of Directors approved the transaction, and the week after I returned from Bogota I was informed that CBN had been given five FM stations in New York state worth $600,000.

By December the FCC had given its approval to the deal, and we fearfully reached out to begin a broadcast service that would extend from Toronto, Canada, to Vermont and Massachusetts, and from the Great Lakes to Pennsylvania. We knew that it was a cold area in more than one way, but when Dede and I joined Scott, Henry Harrison, and Andy Andersen for a prayer meeting at the Wonderland Motel in Ithaca, I was led to the biblical account of Ezekiel at the valley of dry bones.

"That's it!" Scott shouted. "We've got to speak the word and these dead bones are going to come to life."

We teamed Scott with Andy Andersen. They later were joined by Bill Freeman, an outstanding announcer from Kansas City, and finally Larry Black, a Spirit-filled young man who had been a top-rated disc jockey at WPOP in Hartford, Connecticut.

Together they put on the best-sounding Christian radio format I had ever heard. Under the anointing of God, these fellows began to speak God's Word, and sure enough, the dry bones in upstate New York began to stir. In fact, they began to "shake, rattle, and roll."

XXIV

A Limited Figure

At 12:00 noon January 1, 1969, we began broadcasting over the five-station Northeast Network—"CBN Northeast," we called it. At that moment God had multiplied our original three-dollar bank deposit into an operating unit of six radio stations in North America, one radio station in South America, one color television station in Portsmouth, a television permit for Atlanta, and a beautiful headquarters building and production center. Our stations covered 10 million people twenty-four hours a day with the message of Jesus' love.

I was thrilled at what God had done. Some men might have felt content to rest at this point, but a divine discontent was urging me on.

"Pat, can't you arrange a little more time with your family?" Dede remarked one night. "I thought we Christians were supposed to live balanced lives, but how can we when you're gone all the time?"

"We can spend plenty of time together in heaven," I laughed. "Seriously though, Honey, there are 3½ billion people in this world, and we're not scratching the surface. There's so much more to do."

God had told me to claim the world. We had the skilled staff and the technical know-how to reach the world for Jesus. We needed a few more anointed men of God, the necessary equipment, and a great deal of money.

First of all we needed new equipment where we were. The New York stations were underpowered and equipped with antiquated transmitters. To go on the air in Atlanta required a complete television equipment package. In Portsmouth there was a need for an entire television studio and production complex, and I felt I should make good on my promise to raise our power to one million watts.

Our chief engineer, Bill Gregory, and I gingerly considered just a few of the electronic devices required. "Pat, this is going to be brutal," he said. "Are you sure we should get into it?"

"It doesn't cost much to ask questions," I replied. And ask questions he did. The more he asked, the more he realized we lacked. His list grew into many pages.

Finally he came to me and said, "Pat, we can hardly afford to buy new tubes. Are you sure this is right?"

I looked him straight in the face. "Bill, for the past eight years we have limped along from one piece of junk to the next. We have got to reach this country for Christ, and I believe that he will give us everything we need to do his work. Figure everything you need to do the job right."

When the word of our plans got out, equipment salesmen descended upon us like flies onto honey.

Our final negotiation was with RCA. Bill Gregory and the RCA salesmen huddled for about a week, pricing our requirements. They finally brought the price to me. "You'd better sit down," Bill said.

"How much?" I asked, gripping my chair.

"Three million, three hundred thousand."

"Do you mean dollars?" I gasped.

"I certainly do. You said the Lord will supply what we need, and that's what its going to cost."

A surge of faith went through me. "Brother, you are about to see what the Lord can do. First, though, we had better work out a price concession and credit terms."

Ed Tracy, whose parents had been missionaries to Turkey, was the Sales Vice-President for the Broadcast Division of RCA. He arrived in Portsmouth with John Kunkel, the top credit man for the division. We went out to lunch.

"Gentlemen," I told them, "we work under some unusual conditions here, and we need some special credit terms before we can even discuss anything else."

"What do you have in mind?" John Kunkel asked.

Mainly I had in mind the fact that we didn't have any money, and that I didn't want to be obligated unless first God supplied what was needed. I outlined a proposal which would give us a very low down payment, a year's moratorium on payments, a long-term pay out, low interest rates, complete flexibility in the timing of purchases, and a legal escape in case God didn't supply the necessary down payment.

Kunkel fixed me with a bewildered stare, "Pat, on some deals we give on one end, on some we give on the other end, but you have asked for every credit concession we have ever given anybody—all at one time." He paused, then continued with a smile, "But in order to meet the competition, we'll give you what you are asking. But please remember one thing. If you default on this contract, we'll have to sell equipment for the next twenty years just to make up the loss."

I was speechless with joy. Here was the biggest broadcast electronics company in the United States offering us close to $2½ million in credit on what I considered fantastic terms. 1 thrust out my hand and shook his. "Thank you, John," I murmured.

John Kunkel left for Philadelphia, while Ed Tracy remained for the final negotiations. Ed shook his head. "I can't understand John," he said. "You people must really have impressed him. He's one of the toughest credit men in the business, and he gave you everything you asked for."

I smiled. "Ed, it was the Lord." I didn't realize how much the Lord was in it until the meeting continued.

"Pat," Tracy told me, "your order is the sixth largest our company has ever received from a single customer. Bill has selected the very top of the line."

"But Ed," I broke in, "on a package this size we expect some price concessions. We have a limited figure to deal with."

"How much can you spend?" he asked.

I waited. Then the Lord spoke, "Don't go over $2½ million."

"Ed," I said, "our top limit is $2½ million."

As our friendly negotiating continued into the night, I remembered the days in 1960 when Mr. Twohig of RCA and I had wrestled over the $44,000 owed RCA by Tim Bright. Ed Tracy gave a point now and then, and we deleted some items that we could do without. Finally, he said, "Pat, there's one last thing I can do. I'll give you a $58,000 trade on your old transmitter. That will make the deal stand at $2,528,000. I just can't go any lower."

"Ed," I said, "if you can drop the $28,000, we've got a deal."

"Dammit, Pat!" he roared. "You are the most obstinate so-and-so I have ever seen. You win. It's a deal."

He broke into a big smile, walked across the room, and we shook hands.

"Thank you, Lord," I prayed silently. During that evening God had caused Ed Tracy to give us a $600,000 reduction in price to go along with the best credit terms I had ever heard of. I could hardly believe what had happened.

A few days later my phone rang. It was long distance from Dallas, Texas. "Pat, something fantastic has just come up. It's a tremendous opportunity to get the Gospel out." I recognized the voice of Bob Kellum. I had met Bob that winter at a Religious Broadcasters' Convention. He was a Spirit-filled Quaker who had formerly been a transmitter engineer with the Far East Broadcasting Company in Manila. Presently he was serving as United States director of the Central African Radio which operated out of the tiny country of Burundi. Bob Kellum shared my enthusiasm for the Jewish people. When I told him that we had felt that one day God might be calling us to establish a station in Israel, he had made an immediate offer of help. He had promised to visit Continental Electronics in Dallas to get the necessary information about the cost of a super-powered station that would be capable of reaching Russia and the Arab lands from Israel.

"I'm calling from the Continental offices right now," Bob continued. "Just yesterday they repossessed a radio station in Costa Rica. It has one million watts on AM and 50,000 watts on shortwave. It's the most powerful radio station in the Western Hemisphere. How would you like to have it for the Lord?"

"Bob," I replied, "you can't be serious."

"I'm dead serious," he went on. "This station is already built. With a few adjustments it would be ready to go. You could reach 500 million people with it in North and South America, not to mention the shortwave to Europe and Asia."

"It sounds incredible," I exclaimed. "How much would it cost?"

"They're talking a million dollars, but you could probably get it cheaper. They might even give it to CBN for a tax deduction like those stations in New York. But, Pat, more than money, there's the time involved. It would take years to put a station like this together."

I wanted to shout, but struggled to keep calm. "Brother, I'll pray about it. Send me all the information you can, and don't forget the material you promised to get about the Israel station."

God had spoken about the world. Here, it seemed, was his fulfillment. With this station, CBN would be operating the largest Christian broadcasting station in the world. Our little thousand-watt station in Bogota was reaching eight countries. What would a million watts do!

I shared the vision with Jim Bakker. "We must get this station to win souls," he said. Then he continued, "Do you realize that with this station the Christian Broadcasting Network will be a truly international ministry? It could be God's way of giving us support all across America."

Soon more information about the Costa Rican station came from Bob Kellum. It was called La Voz de La Victor. It had been built by a wealthy but eccentric Texan named Bill Windsor. His only explanation for building such a gigantic thing was that "God had told him to do it." So Bill Windsor was the forerunner, who had prepared the way.

Exciting as it was, Costa Rica had to be pushed into the background. I was conducting a tour to Israel, and with me was the plan for a super-powered station to be located near the Dead Sea.

"A friend on the space agency has told me," Bob Kellum wrote, "that satellite photographs have shown that the Dead Sea is the optimum place in the whole world to broadcast into Russia."

Included in Kellum's analysis were budget figures. For what is called a "turnkey" job with a million-watt AM station and a 500,000-watt shortwave station, the cost was $5 million.

The clear moonlight illuminated the Turkish coast as our plane moved rapidly across the Mediterranean. My mind went back to the Bible class I taught to young Jewish couples in Westchester County in 1957; I remembered that Dede and I had felt what we thought was a call to be missionaries to Israel. Somehow I knew that the future of CBN was intertwined with the destiny of the nation of Israel. I didn't know exactly how we would be related, but I did know that the start of construction of our headquarters building on the same day that the Six-Day War began was highly significant. The take-over of Jerusalem by the Jews during that war was a signal that the times of the Gentiles had ended. In my thinking, the ministry of CBN was an end-time ministry. Like John the Baptist, we had been called to proclaim the end of the old age and to prepare the people for the coming of Jesus Christ and the new age.

My musings were cut short by the voice of the Lord. "You are entering into the Holy Land. This is a land of prophetic significance. I have let you make mistakes in Portsmouth and New York. I have let you make mistakes in South America. You must not make mistakes here!"

A sense of awe came over me. Everything that happened in the Holy Land would take on worldwide prophetic import. I felt that God had called me to enter into Israel. His warning was not to be taken lightly.

Only God could open such a door. In the natural it was impossible.

The Israeli government said as much. My first contact was with Dr. Midzini, Director of Press Affairs in Jerusalem. He referred me to an official at the Israeli Bureau of Posts in Tel-Aviv who was friendly, but indicated that he was an engineer not a policy maker. My next contact was with Michael Arnon, Secretary to the Israeli Cabinet. He was interested, and promised careful consideration. I left my proposal with Dr. Midzini for delivery to Michael Arnon.

I returned to Portsmouth. Once it had seemed that no door was open; now doors were open on every side. Calls were coming in for help all across the country. Christian television stations, sparked by what we had been doing, were beginning to take form in many cities. Miami, Greenville, Akron, Pittsburgh, Los Angeles, Indianapolis, Chicago, Dallas—just to name some of the places. I knew that these stations would be calling on us for television programs, and these programs would be expensive to produce and distribute.

Then a TV station in Boston which we had been praying about for years was offered to us at a distress price. Right behind that came the offer to sell WMET-TV in Baltimore. I knew that one day God would use this station to cover the nation's capital with Christian television programs.

Then came the icing on the cake. Radio station WOR in New York City is considered to be the leading radio station in America. It operates on 50,000-watts clear channel, night and day. Its signal covers the most densely populated part of the United States, from Norfolk to Boston. One day as we were praying, Harald Bredesen and I had claimed it for Jesus.

Unexpectedly I received a call from New York. I had answered a blind ad which advertised a television station for sale. My caller was a Vice-President of RKO-General, and he was answering my letter. He wanted to sell a UHF television station in Hartford, Connecticut. "I'm not interested in Hartford," I told him, "but is your company interested in selling any of your other stations?"

"Yes," he said, "we'll sell any of them."

"How about WOR radio?"

"Yes, even that one if you can pay the price—say $30 million. Perhaps we can get together and talk."

That wasn't really talking range, but by faith I viewed the call as an open door.

Then I sat down before the Lord and began to pray and to figure. I had asked God for open doors to reach the world. Each door was open, yet a sentry that looked like a dollar sign was guarding every one.

I did some rapid calculating:

Atlanta	$1,500,000
Boston	1,500,000
Baltimore	1,500,000
Israel	5,000,000
Costa Rica	1,500,000
WOR	30,000,000
Syndicated Programs	1,000,000
	$42,000,000

Forty-two million dollars!

This seemed like a tremendous amount of money. But, I asked myself, was it too much to pay to reach almost one billion people with the Gospel? Was it too much for a ministry to even 200 million people in the United States?

Of course it wasn't too much, I told myself. It wasn't enough! To reach the world, I figured that we would need $100 million. I began secretly to pray for this amount.

It was a seemingly innocent act of self-confidence. It made me feel good inside to realize I had enough boldness actually to ask for that amount. But now I realize that self-confidence, self-reliance, or any other *self* I might depend on gives Satan the opening he is waiting for to step in. And step in he did. Gradually, then with increasing momentum, he led me in a harrowing sequence of events so fantastic that even now their memory numbs my senses.

I pass it on in detail, to demonstrate how God will permit his children to be sifted and shaken so that he might perfect them to the end that they may later, "strengthen their brethren." I pass it on to demonstrate the subtlety of our enemy and his uncanny ability to locate the deep flaws in the character of God's servants. I pass it on to show the eternal truth of Romans 8:28, that God indeed shapes every circumstance for good to them that love him, to those who are called according to his purpose.

XXV

An Angel of Light

———
———

One night on the "700 Club" in March, 1970, my guest was a South African evangelist with a prophetic ministry. We had been talking about the need for additional finances for CBN, and just as we went off the air, he looked at me and said, "Brother, it has just come to me that we should pray for $100 million for CBN."

Since nobody knew that I had begun praying for the identical sum, I decided it was a confirmation that God actually wanted us to have this amount. "Praise the Lord! Let's pray about it."

Nothing else was said about this for several months, but as the burden for world missions increased, so did our need for finances. Most pressing was the need for Costa Rica.

Then, in the fall, I received a call from a man in Virginia Beach, saying that God had told him that the man to put Costa Rica on the air was H. L. Hunt, the Texas millionaire. A few days later, a man from Cincinnati telephoned with the same message.

I had gone to school at Washington and Lee with Hunt's son, Herb, and had met the other son, Bunker, in Dallas just a few weeks before. Other than that, I knew little about the family except that it was one of the wealthiest families in the nation.

Then during our fall telethon, seven months after I had begun to pray for the money, a Chief Petty Officer from the Navy base appeared at the station. He told me he had received a vision in which he saw a funnel-type cloud coming out of the southwest, sucking up wine from our TV tower, and scattering it all over the nation. "There was more," he said. "I saw someone with blond hair, about forty-one or forty-two years of age, appear. He was casually dressed in sport clothes, and it was obvious he was going to become a key in this greater outreach."

Two hours later, as I walked through the back door of our home, Dede said, "You had a phone call from Gene Ryder. He wants you to call him back. It sounded urgent."

Gene Ryder was a member of our board of directors, a former editor with the *New York Times* now living in Boston, and a good friend in Christ. The moment Dede mentioned his name, I identified him with the blond-headed, casually dressed man in the Chief's vision.

"Something wonderful has happened, Pat," Gene said when I got him on the wire.

"What's that, Gene?"

"I believe we're going to get our money to put CBN in Costa Rica," he said enthusiastically. "At least $5 million, maybe ten."

"This is fantastic!" I shouted. "Where from?"

"It's going to sound like a fairy tale," Gene warned. "You know I haven't seen my real father since early childhood when I was adopted by the Ryders. I recently learned that his name is Greathope° and that he is in a nursing home in Texas, dying of brain cancer. He is married to a fifty-three-year-old woman named Lucy, who was the nurse for Mrs. H. L. Hunt prior to Mrs. Hunt's death. I flew to Dallas, was reunited with my father, and talked with my stepmother, who is extremely close to Hunt. She told me that Hunt was a member of the First Baptist Church in Dallas and active in various patriotic ventures, and so I asked her if she thought he would be willing to loan CBN $5 million so we could expand the ministry into Costa Rica."

Gene paused for breath. "Lucy agreed to approach him on the matter and has just called me back. Hunt wants to make an outright gift to CBN of $10 million!"

° The names are fictitious; the events are all too real.

I almost turned cartwheels in the kitchen where I was talking on the phone.

After that, I was on the phone with Gene Ryder in Boston almost daily. He, in turn, was hearing from Lucy Greathope at regular intervals, and finally in December he said, "The amount of money has grown, Pat. The sum is now closer to $40 million that she is going to get for us."

"Gene, I just don't understand. What kind of power does this woman hold over this man?"

"I can't keep this from you any longer, Pat. It wouldn't be fair. Lucy Greathope is actually the illegitimate daughter of H. L. Hunt. That's how I can assure you this money is coming. He's set up a trust for her; the sum is something close to $40 million—and she wants nearly all of it to go to CBN."

"How did all this come to pass?" I asked, astonished.

"At first Lucy didn't know who her father was," Gene said. "Then three years ago her mother was killed in an accident, but she left a letter stating that H. L. Hunt was Lucy's real father. When Lucy confronted Hunt with the letter, he readily admitted having fathered a child. He even joked, saying, 'All these years I thought you were a boy. Now I guess you're going to blackmail me.' "

" 'No,' Lucy told him, 'I don't want any of your money. I just want to be your daughter.' This impressed Hunt, and later he asked Lucy to nurse his wife when she was dying. 'Hap,' as she now calls him, is turning over much of his fortune to her, and she has come to us for legal advice on how to use it for the Lord's work."

How easy it is in retrospect to see that I should have approached such a staggering proposal with extreme caution. But the $40 million seemed to be such a providential answer to prayer that I felt no need to proceed defensively. Yet I was aware that receiving an amount of this nature could be a terrible spiritual snare, so Dede and I agreed that before I made any kind of commitment I should take time away from everything to fast and pray for seven days.

Thus far, no one in Norfolk knew of the situation, although by this time I was beginning to adjust not only my thinking, but my methods of running the stations, as if we already had the money in hand. Though consciously I was unaware of it, no longer did it seem imperative to take the time to check even the most insignificant decisions with the Lord, nor did the little one-, five-, and ten-dollar contributions that had been CBN's lifeblood seem quite so important. And my original insistence that CBN operate wholly on faith, now seemed merely the prelude for God's abundant new provision.

New Year's Day dawned, and as was our custom, the staff met at the station for a day of fasting and prayer. Paul Morris, who had by now joined our staff, was present in the prayer room, and as we waited before the Lord, he spoke up and said, "I have the strongest urge to pray for $100 million for CBN."

Surely Paul's impression could have come only through supernatural revelation. I was ready now to cast all caution to the winds and move out with what someone had called "reckless faith."

That afternoon I rented a hotel room in Norfolk to spend a week in fasting and prayer. I asked the Lord that if this enormous gift did come that I might be kept humble before him, and I asked emphatically, though perhaps a bit reluctantly, that, if this provision was not of him, he would shut the door to it.

Gene Ryder drove down from Boston to spend the night praying at the hotel with me. We asked Paul and Dede to join us. "Brother, this is the final story," Gene said, shaking his head. "Lucy has just heard from Hap that the total amount of the trust fund is $113 million. She wants to give CBN $100 million, but we're not to say a word about it until the deal is finalized."

There it was! The 100 million! Neither Lucy nor Gene had known of my prayer for this exact amount. My knees felt like jelly, and I had to sit down.

"Gene," Dede spoke up hesitantly, "I hate to inject any kind of negative note here, but why does this have to be kept secret? It seems that the things of God should always be open and aboveboard. We should be able to check this out with all those involved."

With uncharacteristic vehemence, he turned on Dede: "Can you imagine what could happen to CBN if all this got out now? Not only would we rob our partners of the blessing of giving, but we would be besieged for handouts!"

I had to agree with Gene's logic. And just then, another point popped into my mind: this was a gift, and if we did too much inquiring, it could get back to Lucy that we didn't trust her. We could very well lose the whole deal.

Ignoring Dede's apprehensive look, Gene turned to me and said, "Lucy is coming to Boston next week. She wants to meet you so we can draw up the final papers for the transfer of funds."

Dede was obviously waiting for an answer from me, but I was too overwhelmed to say anything. She and Paul quietly excused themselves and drove home.

Gene returned to Boston the following day. This was the longest total fast I had ever been on, yet I felt not a trace of hunger. Curiously, I got no clear direction from God during the week, but I sensed peace about the entire matter.

The following week, just before I was to leave for Boston, I came by the station to pick up some papers. "Pat," one of the secretaries said as I hurried through the lobby, "a few minutes ago I was in the bathroom when I heard a voice which I'm sure was the voice of God. It said, 'Underwriter for mammoth project.' What do you suppose that meant?"

I smiled, shrugged my shoulders, and hurried on to catch my plane. But to me, this was one more confirmation from the Lord.

That afternoon I met Lucy Greathope at Gene Ryder's beautiful home in the outskirts of Boston. She was a simple woman, totally lacking in worldly pretense. She bore such a striking resemblance to Bunker Hunt, H. L. Hunt's son, that any lingering doubts I might have had were completely washed away.

That night we sat up until after midnight listening to this humble, uneducated woman tell the fantastic story of her relationship with her natural father.

"Hap came to my apartment Christmas Day," she said, "and we stayed up late that night reading the Bible together. God has brought us into the most beautiful spiritual relationship imaginable, and I want to glorify him by putting this money to work in his kingdom."

I sat across the room from her, enthralled by the obvious sincerity of her story. In times past, I had almost always been able to discern a lie—in fact, I prided myself on how thoroughly I checked situations out—but this time it was so obvious that this woman was telling the truth that it seemed wrong even to question her. My impression was enhanced by Gene's total confidence in his stepmother's story.

"How can we help you?" I asked.

"Write this down," she said, "and work out the details. I want to give $100 million to CBN—no strings attached. It is to be an outright gift, and you can use it in any way you want. I want to give $2 million to evangelist Lester Rolloff in Corpus Christi, $1 million to Oral Roberts University to set up a scholarship fund, $2 million to Gene, and $4 million to his children. The balance, I want set up in a trust fund to support my dying husband and our adopted son who is slightly mentally retarded."

I slept very little that night, spending most of the time sitting on the side of the bed working out the draft for the legal documents necessary to make these arrangements. The next morning we prayed, and Lucy told additional incidents in her relationship with Hunt, all of which added to the credibility of her account.

It was close to noon when Lucy sighed and said, "I guess I should tell you the whole story, since it looks like we're going to be doing business together. This $113 million is in cash, but Hap is also leaving me the controlling interest in the Hunt Oil Company, which is worth about $300 million. The shares have already been endorsed over into my name. Hap is afraid his sons and his sister, Hassie, will quibble with one another when he dies, so he's leaving it in my name with the stipulation that I not sell it. As soon as the stock is mine, I want to put it into a foundation that will help send the Gospel around the world."

A hundred million dollars could do enormous good in God's service, and $300 million more for radio and television would be sufficient to evangelize every creature on earth. It was like a dream come true. I felt like shouting, but somehow, I managed to go back to work that morning around Gene's kitchen table, drawing up plans for the "Worldwide Gospel Foundation"—a foundation which would handle Hunt's vast fortune to the glory of God.

On the way back to the airport, I turned to Gene and said, "What should I do? We'll need a lawyer."

"Yes," he said, "the finest one you can find in Norfolk. Get him to put this together. We'd better do it fast, because Lucy has leukemia and won't live another year."

I returned to Tidewater and retained the best law firm in the area. We went to work on the papers with the attorneys. They put their entire secretarial staff to work on them, and we worked around the clock for more than a week, drawing up wills, trusts, charitable bequests, and foundation papers. We had to check out not only the laws of Texas and Virginia, but all the federal tax forms and schedules as well. Rushing it through, I packed it in my briefcase and took off for Dallas to meet again with Lucy Greathope.

She went over the legal papers with a fine-tooth comb, changing bits and portions here and there and adding legal words at intervals. It was obvious that this uneducated woman was no fool, but had an intimate knowledge of the law as well as an amazingly astute financial brain. Her abilities were almost uncanny, yet throughout she radiated a homespun sincerity and graciousness.

"I want you to meet me next Wednesday at the Chase Manhattan Bank in New York," she said. "Hap has agreed to be there, and we will finalize the plans for the transfer of funds." We prayed together, and I returned to my hotel.

Before leaving Dallas, I negotiated with LTV Electrosystems, the parent corporation of Continental Electronics, for the station in Costa Rica. They now wanted the $1 million in cash before they would turn the station over to us to begin operations. Knowing that

we would have the money in the bank by next week, I shook hands
on the deal and flew back to Norfolk.

For the next week there were daily phone conversations between
Gene, Lucy, and me. She was talking to Hap every day, and he was
ready to make the transfer of the money. There were also several
horrendous crises, narrowly averted, till I felt like I was on a roller
coaster with no safety bar to hang on to.

"Pat," Dede told me one night as I dragged myself into the house
still shaking after a near-tragedy when I thought we had lost all the
money," you're so different lately. If I didn't know you were praying
daily about this whole thing, I would strongly suspect this was an all-
out campaign of Satan to destroy you."

"Honey, the one thing I *don't* need right now is additional bad
news. Let's just forget it for this evening and try to concentrate on
being father and mother to these children."

But I didn't have time to be husband or father, or station manager,
or president of CBN. The size and significance of Lucy's proposed
gift had eclipsed everything else in my life. Future plans had to be
made, and in the process we became deeply committed to an increased budget for our existing ministry. We were reaching out for
new stations in the United States; we had started a news network
and were sending out syndicated radio and television programs. On
top of all this were the bills we had run up with the attorneys and the
travel to Boston and Dallas.

Had I stopped to think, it might have struck me as strange that I
had known no real peace of mind since the whole business began.
But there was no time to think. Every day presented a new crisis.

Plans were changed once again, and I was to meet with Lucy and
Gene in *Dallas* on Friday afternoon. But instead of meeting me at
the bank, Gene came to my hotel room. He seemed strained and
upset. "This woman is grief-stricken for her father," he said. "There
are all kinds of problems between him and his children, and she's
caught in the middle of them. The money just isn't that important,
Pat. What *is* important is the relationship between these two people,

and I frankly think we should back off. I think CBN is too involved. If we get the money, fine; if not, fine."

"Gene, are you out of your mind?" I exploded. "What do you mean, back off? She's come to us for advice! I've spent weeks and weeks of my time. We've run up thousands of dollars of debts. The Costa Rica deal hinges on whether she comes through or not. And you say back off?"

Gene turned on his heel and stomped out, slamming the door behind him. He reopened the door. "Just leave Lucy alone. She has her own problems," he spat out. "I don't want you talking to her anymore."

I didn't know what to do. I turned and sat down on the side of the bed, my head in my hands. What was going on? Why was Gene acting this way? Why had I lost my temper at one of the finest friends I'd ever had? Never in all my life had I felt more hurt and confused. The tension had been unbearable already, and now this.

Lucy called that night. "Pat, I heard what happened this afternoon with Gene," she said. "I don't know what's gotten into him. He's been acting so strange lately. Perhaps it would be better not to discuss these matters with him anymore. You and I can talk about them between ourselves."

My conversation with her calmed my confusion, but I returned to Norfolk, determined that, no matter what, this situation was not going to break up my friendship with Gene.

On Sunday Lucy called and said, "I've got it."

"Got what?" I asked.

"I've got the money. It's been transferred to my name. All the stock and the cash, too."

"Where is it?" I asked.

"The stocks are in a safe-deposit box in a bank in Dennison, and the money is in the Republic National Bank in Dallas. There is only one catch."

"What's that?"

"Hap is afraid of the community property laws in Texas. His lawyer has advised him that it might be possible for my husband's brothers to step in and claim part of the estate. Hap wants all the stocks to remain in my name and says the only way this can be guaranteed is for me to divorce my husband. What do you think I ought to do?"

I was flabbergasted. We were so close—and now this! If I advised her to take the money, she would have to divorce her husband who was dying of brain cancer. At the same time, I would never be able to spend a nickel of the money without knowing that I had been a party to breaking up a home. Yet, if I told her to stay with Gene's father, we'd miss out on what seemed our one great opportunity to spread the Gospel around the world.

"I'll have to pray," I told her. "Gene is coming down to spend the weekend with us, and I'll call you back after talking to him."

"I don't think there's anything to pray about," Gene snapped when I told him the proposition. "How can we be a party to breaking up their home in these final days of their lives? I'm surprised and disappointed that you even considered any possibility other than telling her to stay with her husband and forget about the money."

I called Lucy back that night. "Gene feels strongly that under no circumstances should you divorce your husband; frankly, I don't feel as strongly as he does."

"That's just double-talk," Lucy said. "What should I do? I'm waiting on you to tell me."

I had to make a decision. "Our advice is that you not divorce your husband," I said rather weakly, realizing that this one statement might well destroy my plans for world evangelization by radio and television.

When I hung up and returned to the living room, Gene lit into me. "Pat, you've got the backbone of a jellyfish! Dangle a large sum of money in front of you, and you're willing to advise a woman to get a divorce from her dying husband in order to get it for you."

"Now hold on, Gene!" I said, feeling the heat rising in my face. "That's not so. I just didn't feel as strongly about it as you did."

"You're a vacillating coward!" Gene roared, jumping to his feet, his face livid with rage.

"All right, brother . . ." I said quietly as I rose to my feet, my fists clenched.

Then suddenly it hit me, deep inside, and I realized what was taking place.

"Gene, wait a minute: if Satan wanted to destroy Christian Broadcasting Network, how would he go about doing it?"

"What do you mean?" Gene said, cooling down somewhat and relaxing his hands.

"I mean that first of all he would hold out a sum of money big enough to allow us to do all the good we had ever dreamed of doing. A small sum wouldn't do; it would have to be so much money that every ounce of our being would be challenged by it. He would have to bring us up to it gradually, in stages—$5 million, then $10 million, then $40 million, $100 million, $400 million. Because if he'd started off with that figure, we would have seen through it instantly. So then what happens? If it falls through, we are bitterly disappointed, and our effectiveness is neutralized through resentment and frustration. Or worse still, if the money did come, it would be so tainted that we would feel guilty the rest of our lives for using it. And whether we got the money or not, we would be so divided that we would begin to fight among ourselves and start clobbering one another—" I ran out of breath—"as we are on the verge of doing."

Gene looked sheepish and sat down gingerly on the front edge of the sofa, staring at the carpet.

"Don't you see what this woman is doing? She's bad-mouthing you to me, telling me not to share things with you, and—"

"Is that so?" Gene interrupted.

I nodded solemnly.

"And," he said contemplatively, "she's been doing the same thing to me about you."

"Brother, I think it's high time we took another look at this entire matter. Something's not right."

But incredibly, our suspicions were wiped away the next night when Lucy called, saying, "Everything's great!"

"What do you mean?"

"I went to Hap and told him I wasn't going to divorce Mr. Great-hope. He said, 'I'm glad you won't. I wouldn't have respected you if you had.' It was some sort of test he was putting me through, and now he's satisfied. I get the money anyway; the stock and cash are all mine."

I went into the den where Gene and Dede were talking—and broke the news.

"I don't know what to do now," Gene said. "I'm no financier." Then he added wistfully, "I've always wanted to go off in the Maine woods and write poetry. Maybe that's what I'll do. I've never been more confused in all my life."

Gene returned to Boston that night, and the next day I received another phone call. This time a woman's husky voice on the other end of the line said, "I'm Mrs. Greathope's bodyguard. Her father hired me to look after her. She wants to talk to you for a minute."

There was a pause, and then Lucy's voice came over the phone. "Pat, this is terrible. I've been sued."

My heart began beating wildly in my throat. *How much more can I take, Lord?* "Who sued you?" I stammered out to Lucy.

"The two brothers, Bunker and Herb, and their Aunt Hassie. They've got a court order and sealed the safe-deposit box where the stock is located. They've done the same with the bank account. It's all tied up, and Hap has sent a bodyguard around to protect me. What should I do?"

"Lucy," I said, fumbling for words, "I don't want to stick my nose into this. Gene is very concerned as it is because we're already so involved."

"But I need help. You've got to help me, Pat; I've got no one else to turn to."

"All right. I'll contact Gene, and we'll fly out tomorrow."

I called Gene, and he said he would leave immediately. I told him

I would leave in the morning and would be staying at the Hilton Inn. "Call there when you get things lined up," I said.

I arrived about midday and spent the entire afternoon in the hotel room waiting for Gene's call. At 10:30 P.M. the phone rang. I could barely hear Gene as he whispered into the phone. "Listen, Pat, the bodyguard's here, and I'm really afraid. Something's going on. I don't know what it is, but the bodyguard thinks someone is going to make an attempt on Lucy's life—and maybe on yours and mine too. I'd stay away if I were you."

"Listen carefully, Gene," I said. "We've got to check this thing out before we go one step further. In the morning, I want you to go to the bank where she says she has the safe-deposit box. Get the banker to tell you who got the court order to close the box. If there's no court order, or no box, we'll know something's wrong. Call me tomorrow as soon as you can."

"Okay, Pat," Gene whispered softly. "I think you're right. I'll let you know as soon as I can."

The next morning I got up at 7:30 and went down to the dining room in the motel. There was a line waiting to get in, and since I was impatient, I turned to leave. When I did, I saw a familiar face. The man looked at me as if he recognized me also, but we passed without speaking.

"Don't leave," an inner voice said.

"But it will take me half the morning to get waited on, and I've got to get back to the room," I argued.

"Don't leave."

I got back in line and stood directly behind the man I thought I had recognized, trying my best to remember where I had seen him before. The hostess finally seated me, putting me at a table where I was facing the same man. Suddenly I recognized him. It was Bunker Hunt whom I had met briefly the previous fall in Dallas.

I got up and went over to his table. He immediately recognized me. "Hello, Pat," he said warmly, getting up to shake my hand. "How are things in Norfolk? What brings you to Dallas?"

"Well," I stammered, completely taken off guard and wondering how much he knew of my involvement with Lucy, "I'm here to do business with LTV on a station we're trying to purchase in Costa Rica. How's Herb? I haven't seen him since we played poker together in school."

"He's just fine. Our offices are on the nineteenth floor of the First National Bank Building. Why don't you come up and see him? He'll be glad to see you after all these years."

My meeting with Bunker seemed a sign from the Lord, and, encouraged by it, I went back up to my room to wait for Gene's call. At 2:00 P.M. the phone rang. "Pat, I'm convinced the entire matter is a fraud. It's all a lie."

"Oh, no," I said, sagging into the chair beside the phone. "How do you know?"

"She refused to take me to the bank. She refused to take me to Hunt's house. She was acting funny, and I faced her with the entire thing. I told her I thought she was lying. I said, 'Why me? Why CBN? Why have you done this to us?' A strange, almost weird look came over her face. You know how kind and sweet she is. Well, suddenly all that was gone, and she began raving that she *was* Hunt's daughter and if we didn't believe her she was going to cut us off without a dime. Not only that, but I think this bodyguard is involved in some kind of dope ring."

"Okay, Gene," I managed, struggling to regain my composure. "I ran into Bunker Hunt at breakfast this morning. That *had* to be the Lord! Anyway, he couldn't have been more cordial, and even invited us up to his office to see Herb. I feel we're supposed to go. I'll call for an appointment."

We met promptly at 4:30 P.M. at Herb's office, and I quickly ran through the entire story from the beginning.

"First of all," Herb said, "there is no Lucy Greathope—at least not to my knowledge. My mother died in the Mayo Clinic ten days after she got sick, and there was no Mrs. Greathope who nursed her. However, let me call just to make sure."

He made a phone call and confirmed that there was no Mrs. Greathope who had nursed his mother. We continued to ask about other details in her story, one after another of which seemed to check out with frightening accuracy. At that point, we weren't sure who to believe, and Gene was almost finished with our story.

"So when she told us that you, Bunker, and your Aunt Hassie had filed suit against her—"

"Aunt Hassie?" Herb grinned. "Would you believe Hassie is my father's brother?"

"Oh no!" Gene said, slumping in his chair. "She thought Hassie was a woman. She's made the whole thing up from bits and fragments of information gathered here and there."

I looked at Gene. "No, I don't think she was making it up, nor do I think she went around picking up bits of information. She got this story from the master liar himself."

Herb said, "I'm sorry. People claim these things all the time. My father may not be everything everyone wants him to be, but one thing he doesn't have is an illegitimate daughter. Wealthy people get hit with paternity suits constantly, and it's not unusual for things like this to spring up. I'm just sorry you guys got sucked into it."

So it was all a fraud. There was no money. No stock transfer. No safe-deposit boxes. Nothing. There was to be no big deal. No giant foundation. There was to be no quick and easy way for me to evangelize the world, anymore than there had been a quick and easy way for Jesus. Satan had offered to lay all of the kingdoms of the world at his feet. Jesus had wisely rejected Satan's offer, choosing instead a way of suffering, rejection, and crucifixion. Unfortunately, I had been foolish enough to believe that my Lord's example did not apply to me.

We returned home, sick, brokenhearted—and chastened. Gene, who had quit his job, went back to New England to pull his life together. I returned to Norfolk to try to pick up the pieces of a shattered dream.

My entire being was spent and exhausted. It did not seem that I could ever rise to another challenge again. Yet for the first time in months, I sensed again the abiding presence of the Holy Spirit. Deep inside I could have wept for joy. The Lord loved me enough to let me learn a lesson I would never forget. I could only pray that the price for my lesson would not be the breakup of CBN.

XXVI

Back to Bethel

———
———
———

"Now what?" Dede said, smiling to cheer me up as she pulled the car out of the airport parking lot and turned into the heavy traffic on Little Creek Road.

I sat slumped down in the seat beside her. "It's still God's venture," I said. "He knew he was dealing with a lump of clay when he chose me. But from now on, if he wants CBN to expand, he'll have to do it."

We drove silently for a while as I remembered a passage of Scripture I had read on the plane coming in from Dallas.

"There comes a time in every man's life when he is called back to Bethel," I murmured.

"What do you mean?" Dede asked, keeping her eyes on the road as she turned the station wagon onto Tidewater Drive and headed toward Norfolk.

"In Genesis 35, God told Jacob to arise and go up to Bethel—back to the place where he made his first vows to God. God said that before he could bless him, he would have to put away any false idols and renew those old vows."

"But Pat, you haven't set up any false idols. There was no compromise involved. This was simply a gift from a nice old lady. I was taken in by it, too. I'm a nurse and should have recognized psychotic delusions when I saw them, but this woman was different. No, I don't think you've set up any false idols."

"Yes, I have," I said straightening up. "I've been planning as though I were the President of NBC not CBN—and spending like it, too. I was in such a hurry to be big that I left God's best, but praise the Lord, he's never left us. Dede, I'm going to call all our old original staff together, and we're going to rediscover and renew our initial objectives and purposes . . . starting by closing the door where Satan got in."

"The first thing I want to do is admit I was wrong—terribly wrong," I told the staff after sharing the entire story with them. "In the very beginning, God told me to walk by faith and not by sight. Now we're going to return to that. Somehow we've lost sight of our original goals, but praise God, he's taught me that if we don't walk by faith, then it's possible that he just might let us have it all by ourselves. He'll take his hands off the station, and even though we might become a financial success, we'd be a spiritual failure."

Jim Bakker spoke up, his voice quivering. "Pat, I've got to apologize to you. A month ago the Lord spoke to me and told me that one of the ones you had been trusting for spiritual guidance was being used of Satan to feed you bad advice. I'm sorry, but I was afraid to tell you."

I thanked him and winced inwardly at how unapproachable I must have become.

John Gilman, our production manager, raised his hand. "I've got a confession to make, too. Last Wednesday when you were on your way out of here for Dallas, I received a message from the Lord. He told me to tell you, but I didn't because it didn't seem to make any sense. The message was, 'Beware of everything you say that it be in the Spirit, for a woman is going to deceive you.' "

I felt tears welling up in my eyes and silently thanked God for showing me that even in the darkest part of the valley, he had been in charge of the situation, seeing that no permanent harm would befall me.

For years we had tossed the words "professional" and "spiritual" around the station as if they were opposites. Many of our broadcasters had indicated that CBN wasn't "professional" enough. Now, in the light of what had happened, we sensed that God was calling us back to our original spiritual concepts, even if it meant becoming unprofessional. How can you worry about technical production when the cameraman is caught up in the Spirit and begins to weep over someone's testimony? How can you be professional when you pray for someone to rise up and walk in Jesus' name? Professionalism always watches the clock. Now God was calling us back to a concept that says, "Who cares about the time if God is moving?"

"All of you need to understand that we are on the brink of financial disaster," I told the staff as we got ready to leave. "This entire operation could go down the tubes tomorrow should the Lord choose to remove his grace. But now I'm beginning to believe that this is the way God intends it—all of us leaning on Jesus."

The greatest discovery of all was that CBN was primarily dependent, not on money, but on prayer. Had we come into the $100 million that Satan had dangled before us, we would have immediately lost all our small contributors who would have rightly reasoned, "Why should we sacrifice and give our money when CBN has all the money it needs?" They would have lost a real opportunity to help in God's work, and we would have lost the thing we depended upon more than anything else: their prayer support.

The staff meeting ended in a note of victory, and when I was alone, I began to think. It just may be that we had rediscovered one of God's almost forgotten principles: God never operates by hatching golden eggs. Rather, he wants his people to grub, scratch, and walk by faith, for it's in the grubbing and scratching that they plant the seeds which will bear the fruit of the Spirit. I was reminded of that seventy dollars I had in my pocket when we moved to Tidewater and realized that God's greatest experiences are always incubated in lack of funds, lack of self-ability, lack of self-anything.

There came to my mind a message God had given to me through Harald Bredesen some time ago: "Your early ministry seems small in your eyes now. The time will come when this present ministry will seem just as small when you compare it to the place that I will take you." Suddenly I remembered my bitter disappointment almost ten years before when Mr. Dangler had deceived me with an offer of funds. God had used that bitter experience to teach and mold me in preparation for the greatest opportunity of my life. Now, ten years later, I knew deep inside that the bitterness and disappointment with Lucy Greathope was God's prelude to a whole new level of ministry. Faith surged inside me, and I spoke into the empty room: "Devil, you have thrown every weapon you've got at me, and praise God you have lost!"

Late that evening, I sat alone in the quiet prayer chapel. My eyes moved from the dark red carpet to the uncut crystal boulder in the center of the room, to the Bible that lay on top of it, and on up to the suspended wooden cross. The door leading out to the lobby was closed, and I felt the presence of the Holy Spirit permeate every corner of the room.

I slipped off the circular bench and knelt before the big white and gray rock whose thousands of facets gently sparkled, reflecting the soft light from the ceiling. Over my head was the cross, and directly in front of me was the open Bible.

I started to pray and to thank God for dealing with me as hard as I needed to be dealt with and for not releasing me until the lesson had sunk home. I asked his forgiveness . . . and accepted it . . . and re-committed my life to his plan, vowing total submission. As I prayed, my attention was drawn to something lying on top of the Bible, directly under the bottom of the cross. It was a typed sheet of paper, and I picked it up, recognizing it as the prayer-request list placed there every day by the secretary. I began to read:

Pray for a sister who has a brain hemorrhage. Unconscious five days.

Pray for a grandson in Vietnam.

Pray for a man who wants to commit suicide.

Pray for a woman who, if God doesn't intervene, will kill herself.

Pray for a young wife with throat cancer—dying.

Pray for two sons who are alcoholic.

Pray for a Norfolk policeman, shot, critical.

Pray for a baby run over by a truck.

Pray for a woman with four children in desperate financial need . . .

On and on I read. There were more than fifty of them, requests that had been called in that day and placed between the Bible and the cross where all who entered could pray.

"That's your purpose," the Lord said softly as the tears streamed down my cheeks. "That's why I've put you here, to minister to my little ones, to give a cup of cold water in my name."

Through the tears I looked at the Bible and saw the words of Jesus:

The Spirit of the Lord is upon me,
because he hath anointed me to preach
the gospel to the poor;
he hath sent me to heal the brokenhearted,
to preach deliverance to the captives,
and recovering of sight to the blind,
to set at liberty them that are bruised,
to preach the acceptable year of the Lord.